Wild Seed Pro[...] within ancest[...] and Wabanaki territory now called Maine.

We recognize the inherent sovereignty of the tribes where we live and work, the Wabanaki, the People of the Dawn: the Houlton Band of Maliseet Indians, the Mi'kmaq Nation, the Penobscot Nation, and the Passamaquoddy Tribe. We support their continued work for justice, self-determination, and decolonization.

The work of Wild Seed Project is necessary precisely because of the ongoing violence of settler colonialism. The exploitative practices of European colonizers, which continue to this day, are directly responsible for the displacement of the native plants that form the foundation of local food webs that we are working to restore.

What does it mean to build and rebuild reciprocal relationships with people, plants, fungi, soil, water, and air? Reestablishing resilient ecosystems in which all forms of life can thrive is one piece of deconstructing a colonial legacy.

As we do our work at Wild Seed Project, we are clear: this knowledge and information did not start, nor will it end, with us. The resources we share are from many generous teachers, both human and nonhuman. We are committed to ongoing learning and growth, and encourage you to join us in learning more about the historical and present-day relationships of Indigenous communities to the place you live (native-land.ca), and in supporting Indigenous-led efforts to protect the land, water, plants, and creatures among us.

Contribute to Healing
The mission of Wabanaki REACH is to "support the self-determination of Wabanaki people through education, truth telling, restorative justice, and restorative practices in Wabanaki and Maine communities." Learn more and support their work at **www.wabanakireach.org**.

This land & knowledge acknowledgment is a living document.
We welcome your feedback: **info@wildseedproject.net**.

Gardening for Biodiversity

Native Plants for the Northeast

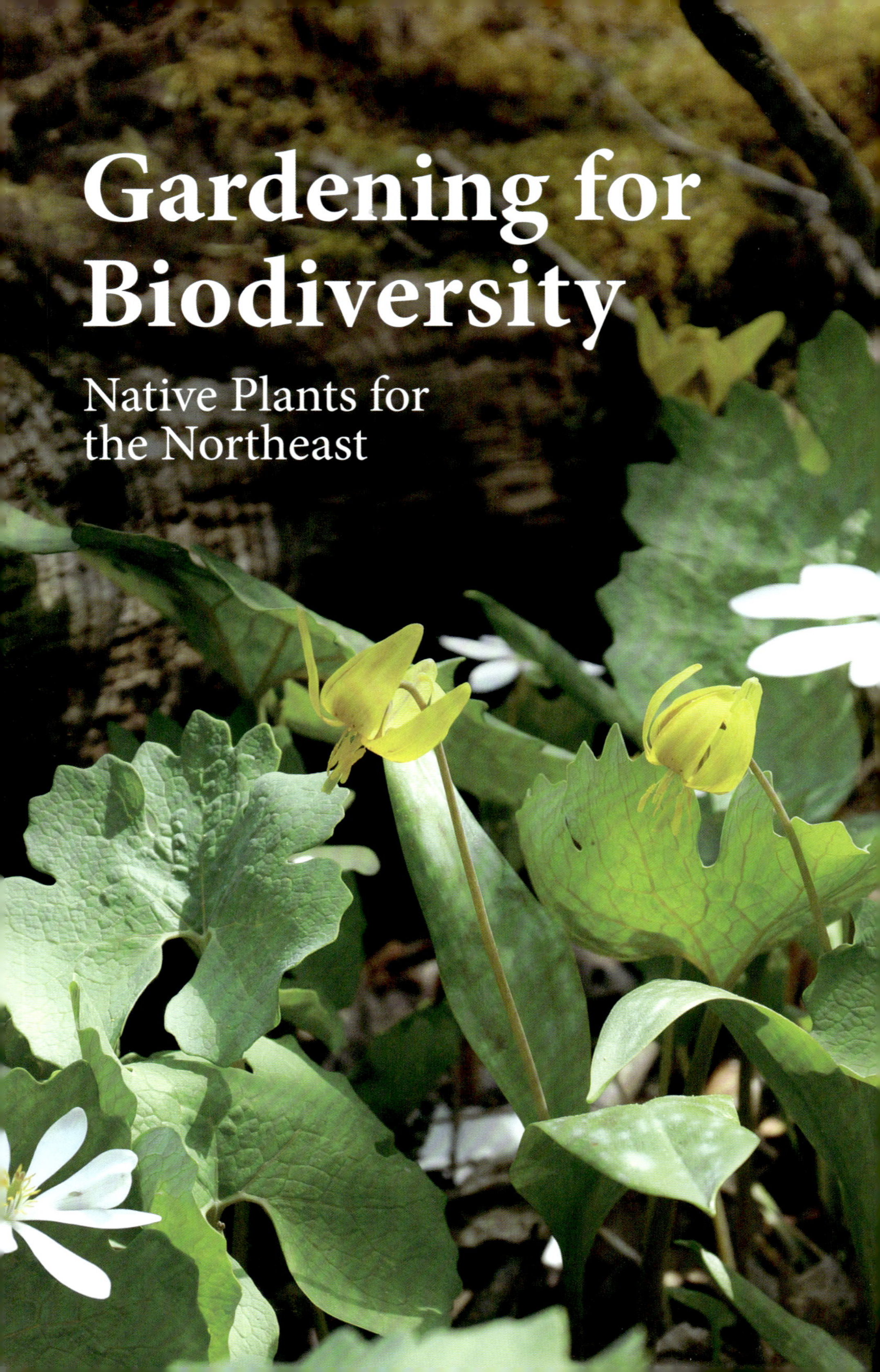

On Diversity in the Time of Disaster

by **JESS GILDEA**

In a biodiverse system, every organism has a part to play: each with its own orientation, its own strategy for survival, honed over generations, all knit together to form a functioning and thriving community. Each is attuned to the availability of resources. Some adapt to make use of less, others to make use of the things no others can. This diverse multiplicity of adaptations benefits both the individual and the collective whole, creating a looping symphony of stress and adaptation, decay and new life.

As this book comes together in January 2025, the city of Los Angeles is on fire. A few months ago, in September, Hurricane Helene devastated southern Appalachia. At this time last year, Vermont was underwater. Where hope is hard to hold in the face of cascading disasters—slippery and demanding—persistence is sturdy, reliable. Persistence is a practice.

We keep sowing the seeds, knowing they may wash away.

We keep putting plants in the ground, though there is smoke in the air.

We keep expanding our understanding of community beyond our human connections and the built environment to include the vast, glittering diversity of life on this planet, including all those under threat and pushed to the margins, and every little thing underfoot.

We keep counting and caring for the ones who find us—the spotted leopard moths and the katydids and the woodcocks and the leafhoppers—though our future is wildly unknown.

This persistence becomes a prayer.
We keep at it. We let our roots run deep as we transform our communities—our backyards and farms and schools and libraries—into sanctuaries for the storms to come, beacons for an ecological future that may be battered but is not yet lost.

Contributed Essays

The following contributed articles share a range of perspectives on the profound importance of diversity in building community, adaptability, and resilience. As you read these essays, we invite you to consider these values through both an ecological and cultural lens. We hope that the words shared by our contributors prompt reflection and discussion of the "what, how, and why" of diversity, well beyond our gardens' borders.

Wild Seed Project values learning through conversation, and we view these essays as part of a larger dialogue about the importance of diversity in all walks of life. Language, ideas, and knowledge evolve through discourse. As we learn from one another, we grow more resilient and connected as individuals and community.

Protective Life

by MEG MITCHELL

In the cozy corner of a community hub in Western Maine, farmers gathered last spring to share their concerns, needs, and strategies for coping with climate change.

Surrounded by unwrapped packages of grilled sandwiches and the warmth of mutual trust, we joked candidly about human extinction and the reality that all our angst and troubles will one day become compressed into a few inches of plastic and steel in the Earth's crust. Whether or not our species thrives, the Earth will eventually be unbothered by the thorn that is extractive capitalism. The fiery substance of Earth's creative cycles will envelope our mortal efforts to live as individuals; flora and fauna will reign benevolently, and the flamboyant perfection of genetic mutations will churn out wonderfully weird expressions of life beyond our wildest visions.

In the meantime, it is our responsibility as farmers and caretakers to soften the blow of the violent and extractive systems of capitalism. In her newest book, *The Serviceberry*, visionary author and Potawatomi botanist Robin Wall Kimmerer suggests that incremental change and creative disruption can help create new systems centered around abundance and reciprocity. We can make these changes on the edges and tears of our status quo.

As farmers in Maine contemplate climate resilience, we find protection in systems that support a diversity of life. Multi-species hedgerows shelter farmsteads from intense wind pressures, resist erosion, feed pollinators, and provide cozy habitat for a fox and her pups. A mix of winter cover crops shelters the soil from pounding rains, nourishes microbial life, and provides sustenance for next summer's crops. Coexisting with a diverse web of species keeps us safe.

Our hearty group of farmers parted from our climate conversation last spring by sharing ways that we mentally cope. Creative dreaming, singing, walks with loved ones, games, and jokes. By bringing what makes us uniquely human into our relationship with the richness of the natural world, we can build and belong in a vibrant future where we all thrive.

MEG MITCHELL began as an apprentice on an organic vegetable farm in 2005 and has been raising produce ever since, working with local markets, planning for financial and climate resilience as well as participating in a network of mutual aid organizations. Meg works to connect farmers with technical support and funding for climate-smart practices and organic transition. Removing barriers to access for communities historically underserved by the Maine Organic Farmers and Gardeners Association (MOFGA) is central to this work, as is integrating emotional resilience into outreach and technical support.

The Corruption of Diversity: Celebrating Exuberant Life

by **BANU SUBRAMANIAM**

Diversity is again under attack—in the realms of nature and culture. All migrants (plants, animals, and humans) are increasingly regarded with suspicion of harming national security, health, and economies. Biodiversity is good only if it is a diversity of desirable species. Foreign species are reviled and, if invasive, eradicated. But foreignness is not absolute. Most agricultural produce is not native. Some foreign species—tumbleweed, cherry blossoms, Georgia peach—have, in fact, been embraced as American icons. European or 'white' immigrants are welcomed in contrast to 'brown' and 'black' immigrants. In short, our views of diversity are grounded in nationalism, shaped by race and gender. Rather than natural or cultural, our views are ideological.

Similarly, consider plant reproduction. Society largely talks in binary terms—male and female plants, flowers or parts of flowers. It also views plants entirely in a heterosexual register. In fact, historians argue that plants have been rendered in the image of Victorian gentlemen and ladies! But plants are imaginative. Most do not reproduce sexually, and when they do, reproduce very differently than humans. More than eighty-five percent of flowering plants are bisexual, producing pollen and seeds within the same flower. Many also vary their timing of production of fertile pollen or ovules. Consider the bush tomato, *Solanum plastisexum*, a gender-fluid plant that is female, male or bisexual at different times. Our binary categories of male and female, and our compulsory heterosexuality, do not fit plants or animals—or, indeed, humans! Rather than natural or cultural, our views are ideological.

Why and how did we arrive here? Colonial histories shaped the disciplines, creating specialized silos that separated the study of nature and culture. If we refuse this separation and think naturecultrually, our ideological biases become starkly visible. The world has immense possibilities. Let us invent new languages, frameworks, and theories to celebrate our exuberant life!

BANU SUBRAMANIAM is a Luella LaMer Professor of Women's and Gender Studies at Wellesley College, plant evolutionary biologist, and author of *Botany of Empire: Plant Worlds and the Scientific Legacies of Colonialism*, among other works.

4
3
5
2
1

Frankie Toan,
Holding Living Things, 2020.
Photo Credit: Wes Magyar

Queer Ecologies and Natural Transformativity

by NICOLE SEYMOUR

In an undergraduate course I teach called Queer Literature and Theory, one concept tends to resonate most strongly with my students: the idea of queer ecologies. Students are particularly struck by the idea of transformation as a natural process, and how this relates to queer human lives—including their own.

As a class, we discuss queer ecologies as a framework that considers the intersection of queer issues and environmental issues. For example, heteronormative biases in science have long suppressed knowledge of homosexual and transexual behavior among nonhuman animals. Queer people are more heavily impacted by climate disasters than non-queer people. Queer people are also statistically more likely to support pro-environmental policies—despite the many efforts by far-right forces to, rather ironically, frame LGBTQ+ people as "unnatural."

The example that really grabbed my students' attention this past semester came from "Rock Jenny," a short story by Callum Angus. The titular character goes through several gender transformations before turning into a rock and, eventually, the moon. One of my students pointed out that the moon is ever-changing, with eight phases that repeat roughly every month. Angus' use of this non-teleological example makes an important intervention into the field of trans literature, which has historically presented transitioning as a "one-and-done" process from male to female or vice versa.

Our class embraced how the story implies that humans—like nonhuman members of the natural world—are everchanging. That it's okay to revise your life story if you realize you're pansexual after initially coming out as bisexual, or if you decide you're nonbinary after first coming out as trans. It's okay to not actually know what you are yet, and to explore your identity.

Transformativity is adaptive and it's all around us, from plants that evolved to be shorter in windy climates to tree saplings that grow larger, light-collecting leaves in the forest understory. Indeed, as Wild Seed Project put it in their 2024 guide, "Static gardens are not resilient gardens."

DR. NICOLE SEYMOUR lives on Tongva Territory in what is now called Long Beach, California. She is Professor of English and Graduate Advisor for Environmental Studies at California State University, Fullerton. She is the author of several books, including *Bad Environmentalism: Irony and Irreverence in the Ecological Age* (University of Minnesota Press) and *Glitter*, an environmental cultural history of that substance (Bloomsbury, "Object Lessons" book series).

Transitional Choices

by **CALLUM ANGUS**

One of the reasons I find transition to be a useful lens through which to look at climate change and our relationship with the environment is that transition requires choice. Transition posits the self as the site of change made with agency to your body, your name; every way in which you live your life completely changes. It requires a split, a divergence, and a figuring out how to live outside the norm and against the mainstream. The scale of this complete and total reworking of one's life is, I think, similar to that which will be required of us to keep living and loving in a time of climate apocalypse.

I've never been comfortable seeking justification from nature for the ways that I am. This approach treats the natural world as separate from myself, from people, and as a kind of buffet of different ways of being. The different species; the plants with many genders, no genders; the creatures who can change genders in what many read as a perfect analogue for the naturalization of a trans identity—all this is endlessly interesting, but it doesn't feel like it gives me permission to exist. Poet Cecilia Vicuña, in *Deer Book*, encapsulates what feels to me like a better approach:

"The flower is the plant's sex, the poem is language's sex. Pollen is the exhalation of the flower. The poem the exhalation of the author."

Light and speech and exhalations: the primordial soup from which we came, and the elements through which we practice loving each other and the lands we inhabit. Difference and diversity is not found in who we are or who we love, but in how we each respond differently to the elements and challenges surrounding us. Vicuña reminds us that it's plants that are the original intermediaries between us and the land, and we would do well to remember that we grow and thrive under much the same conditions that they do. The small queer choices we make now in living right or wrong, the native plants we sow, and the ecosystems we nourish are what coalesce into transition on a planetary scale.

CALLUM ANGUS is a trans writer and editor living in Portland, Oregon, where he edits the literary journal *smoke and mold*, teaches writing workshops online and in-person, and is at work on a novel. He is the author of the story collection *A Natural History of Transition*.

Opening Chapters

The Many Dimensions of Diversity

In the face of great environmental uncertainty, biodiversity is more important than ever to help mitigate risk and build resilience

by **TYLER REFSLAND**

From the crimson petals of a cardinal flower to the velvety stems of sumac, native plants have evolved an astonishing diversity of shapes, colors, lifestyles, and chemistries over the course of millions of years. Collectively, this diversity represents deep-rooted adaptations to a constantly changing world; adaptations that help native plants survive with variable resources and coexist alongside neighboring plants, animals, and microbes.

Among these vast and striking differences, however, many native plant species also share characteristics in common. The healthiest of communities, or groups of species, are those that contain a mix of similarities and differences. Ecologically speaking, these are:

Functionally complementary **communities:** Diverse collectives that are stronger than the sum of their individual parts.

Functionally redundant **communities:** Collectives with broad overlap in ecological roles, diminishing the reliance on any one species.

Together, a mix of *complementarity* and *redundancy* in a landscape helps local ecosystems withstand extreme weather, habitat loss, pests, pathogens, and other unpredictabilities of a rapidly changing world.

How to Promote Biodiversity and Build Resilient Landscapes

Rather than simply crowding in as many native plant species as possible in your own garden, we recommend you familiarize yourself with the **Dimensions of Diversity** (described below) to establish both *complementarity* and *redundancy* among your plantings. By choosing species with a range of differences and overlap in lifestyle, pollination, and defense strategies, you can help build a hedge against an uncertain future.

1 Plant Lifestyles

Plants have evolved a variety of strategies to allocate resources to reproduction, growth, and survival. These strategies govern how plants respond to stress and interact with one another. Each resource-allocation strategy—or"lifestyle"—falls somewhere within a three-sided continuum:

Early establishers
Invest in reproduction

Although often maligned as "weeds," early establishers are shade-intolerant opportunists that play an important ecological role in gardens. They are prolific self-seeders that are adapted to disturbance and are well suited to rapidly stabilize soil. As a bonus, early establishers are often annuals or biennials that bloom in their first or second year.

Keen competitors
Invest in growth

These vigorous plants invest in rapid growth and can shape the physical structure and microclimate of a garden. Often large herbaceous or woody perennials, keen competitors can grow toe-to-toe with many non-native, aggressive plants. Some species may only be suitable for larger landscapes.

Resourceful scavengers
Invest in survival

These are tough plants that invest in survival by doing more with less. Resource scavengers are often small, slow growers adapted to resource-limited environments. Depending on the species, scavengers can tolerate a range of stressors including shade, drought, salt, and low-nutrient or acidic soil conditions.

2 Pollination Strategies

The co-evolution of flowering plants and their pollinators has produced a vast diversity of flower shapes, colors, rewards, and fragrances that effectively attract various generalist pollinators, as well as specialist pollinators that depend on a very limited number of native plant species for food.

Bowl-shaped flowers are radially symmetrical, shallow, and simple. They are displayed in various ways, from single flowers to wide, flattened clusters (umbels). Their floral rewards are accessible to a wide range of pollinators, including sprightly flies and blunderous beetles. ***Examples:*** *cherries, dogwoods, magnolias, roses, viburnums, spiraeas, angelicas, anemones, bloodroot, golden Alexanders, marsh marigold, and wild strawberry.*

Composite flowers characterize members of the sunflower family (Asteraceae), the most species-rich plant family in the Northeast. Although Asteraceae flower heads often resemble individual, daisy-like flowers, they are actually dense clusters of many small flowers called florets. Pollinators of all stripes relish these florets for their plentiful nectar that is portioned out over many weeks. To prevent pollen over-consumption, many Asteraceae species produce hard-to-digest pollen grains that only specialist bees can tolerate. ***Examples:*** *asters, blazing stars, bonesets, coneflowers, and goldenrods.*

Bilabiate flowers have long, narrow, tube-shaped entrances that end with a nectar reward. As a bee backs up to exit a blossom, the upper "lip" of the flower dusts pollen on the pollinator's back. This minimizes the amount of pollen the bee can harvest and maximizes the chances of cross-pollination at the next flower. Bilabiate blooms have corolla tubes that range from short and widely accessible (e.g., mountain mints), to long, narrow, and accessible primarily to hummingbirds (e.g., cardinal flower and scarlet beebalm). Often also visited but less effectively pollinated by nectar-seeking butterflies and moths. ***Examples:*** *mints, beardtongues, irises, and jewelweeds.*

Banner, wing, and keel flowers are characteristic of the pea family (Fabaceae). These butterfly-like flowers each contain three petal types—the banner, wing, and keel. Floral rewards rest deep within the keel petal; bumble bees are amongst the few pollinators strong enough to pry open the keel. ***Examples:*** *redbud, partridge pea, milk vetch, sundial lupine, tick-trefoils, yellow wild indigo, wild senna, and wisterias.*

Spurred flowers of species in the fumitory subfamily (Fumarioideae) share some similarities with banner, wing and keel flowers. Bumble bees and other long-tongued bees must push their heads between the outer and inner petals to reach nectar in the spurs. ***Examples:*** *Allegheny vine, Dutchman's breeches, pink corydalis, and wild bleeding heart.*

Wind-pollinated flowers have no need to attract pollinators. Their flowers are often small, nectarless, and unadorned with color or scent. Although not reliant on animals for pollination, wind-pollinated plants are nevertheless visited by pollen-seeking bees and syrphid flies. Most importantly, their foliage provides food for larvae of numerous butterfly and moth species. ***Examples:*** *birches, oaks, pines, grasses, and many disturbance-adapted plants* (*e.g., plantain, dock, ragweed, mugwort, and nettle*).

Urn-shaped flowers have fused petals that form an enclosed globe with a narrow mouth. This constricted opening is most accessible to bees, including many pollen specialist species. In the urn-shaped flowers of blueberry and cranberry, pollen is locked away in the anthers and accessible only to bumble bees and solitary bees capable of buzzing at just the right frequency to shake out the reward. ***Examples:*** *bearberry, huckleberry, maleberry, and wintergreen.*

Milkweed flowers are unique both in their form and their function. Unlike most flowers, these blooms do not produce loose pollen. Instead, they package their pollen in waxy sacs tucked within a crown of nectar-filled hoods. As insects scurry from one hood to the next for nectar, their legs often slip and get tangled with the pollen sacs. They then carry these pollen sacs to the next plant, facilitating cross-pollination. Milkweeds attract a tremendous range of nectar-seekers including bees, wasps, flies, butterflies, and the occasional hummingbird.

Tube-shaped flowers restrict nectar access to long-tongued pollinators like hummingbirds, butterflies, moths, and long-tongued bees. These blooms often combine with other shapes and forms; flowers with tube-shaped corollas may have openings shaped as a bowl (e.g., phlox), funnel (e.g., azaleas), or composite (e.g., Joe-Pye weed). ***Other examples:*** *bluets, Culver's root, evening primrose, and trumpet honeysuckle.*

3 Defense Strategies

Plants are skilled chemists, capable of crafting a staggering range of phytochemicals to deter herbivory. Specialist herbivores have evolved their own set of counter-defenses to overcome these deterrents, occasionally repurposing plant toxins for their own benefit. Millennia of back-and-forth interactions between herbivores and host plants have diversified both groups. In your garden, you can provide food for a diverse range of generalist and specialist herbivores by planting species with a variety of physical and chemical defenses.

Tough leaves are fibrous and difficult to digest. Many trees and shrubs invest in tough foliage, especially those with long-lived evergreen leaves. Hundreds of species of butterfly, moth, and sawfly larvae circumvent these defenses by mining, windowpane feeding, and skeletonizing leaves to munch only the most palatable parts. ***Examples:*** *cedars, junipers, hollies, rhododendrons, bearberry, and wintergreen.*

Abrasive foliage contains sharp deposits of silica that make leaves largely unpalatable and undigestible. Common in native grass and sedge species, abrasive leaves are effective deterrents of many leaf- eating insects and slugs. However, grasshoppers and skipper larvae have developed mandibles strong enough to mow down even the toughest silica-rich grasses. ***Examples:*** *Canada wild rye, little bluestem, and fringed sedge.*

Prickles, thorns, and spines act to deter or slow down larger herbivores such as rodents and deer. ***Examples:*** *prickly pear cacti, hawthorns, thistles, roses, blackberries, and raspberries.*

Hair-like trichomes grow on most plants, and often serve as a first line of defense against herbivory. Trichomes obstruct insects from moving, eating, or laying eggs; some also secrete sticky resins or irritating chemicals to further slow predation. ***Examples:*** *velvety stems of staghorn sumac; the woolly surface of cinnamon fern fiddleheads; the sticky-hairy leaves of wild blue phlox; and the bristly stems of Rudbeckia.*

Terpenes are naturally occurring volatile chemicals that produce the familiar aromas of citrus, lavender, and pine. Once released, these aromas not only help dissuade herbivory, but also advertise the presence of herbivores to potential predators and parasitoids. Some terpenes can deter a certain degree of herbivory while still remaining attractive to specialized insects. ***Examples:*** *terpenes crafted by bee-balm, sweetfern, and spicebush deter most mammals while attracting larvae of the hermit sphinx moth, dagger moth, and spicebush swallowtail, respectively.*

Phenols are a large group of chemicals that produce the astringency characteristic of unripe fruit, tea, and red wine. Native trees and shrubs use a specialized suite of phenols, including tannins, to defend against leaf-chewing insects. In response, larvae of hundreds of species of butterfly, moth, and sawfly have evolved to feed on only a select set of plant families. ***Examples:*** *several species of brush-footed butterfly and Saturniid moth larvae have adapted to the high levels of tannins and toxic salicylates found in willow leaves.*

Promoting Genetic Diversity, One Seed at a Time

by **TYLER REFSLAND**

Purple and white varities of eastern waterleaf (*Hydrophyllum virginianum*).

Genetic diversity develops over many thousands of years through genetic mutations, migrations, and the reshuffling of genes that takes place during sexual reproduction. The result? A vast spectrum of stark to subtle differences in the growth rate, size, bloom color, flowering time, and tolerance of temperature extremes amongst native plants.

Although not always apparent to the naked eye, such variations within a species are just as important to sustaining local food webs and building climate resilience as variation across species.

Genetically distinct populations may be categorized as subspecies, varieties, or ecotypes depending on how visibly different and geographically isolated they are from other populations—with ecotypes considered the least visibly different and isolated. When shopping for native plants to sow and grow, gardeners most frequently encounter ecotypes. Though these show only subtle variations in appearance, ecotypes contain an array of stress-tested adaptations that shape the plant's growing requirements. Take switchgrass (*Panicum virgatum*) for example. This native perennial grows from the Atlantic Coast to the Great Plains and has at least three ecotypes across this range: one sod-forming type that thrives in the warm, wet lowlands of the southern U.S.; one bunch-forming type accustomed to the cold, dry uplands of the Midwest; and one intermediate type adapted to the salt-laden dunes and marshes of the Atlantic Coast.

Upland (left) and lowland (right) ecotypes of switchgrass (*Panicum virgatum*).

Spring beauty miner bee collecting pollen from a Virginia spring beauty (*Claytonia virginica*) with pink color morph flowers.

A white Virginia spring beauty morph.

Why is genetic diversity important in a rapidly changing world?

Increasing the genetic diversity of native plants in your landscape helps broaden the range of tolerated growing conditions; strengthens local food webs; and cultivates resilience to a range of stressors including extreme weather, herbivory, non-native pests, and pathogens.

Genetically diverse wildflower populations, for example, often stagger their bloom times, which helps maintain synchrony between flowers and pollinators as the climate changes. In the case of the Virginia spring beauty (*Claytonia virginica*)—a charming spring ephemeral native to the eastern U.S.—bloom times vary with the color of the blossoms, with white color morphs flowering earlier than pink color morphs in response to earlier springtime thaws. Such variation gives the flower's specialist pollinator—the spring beauty miner bee—a fighting chance of finding pollen as the onset of springtime becomes more unpredictable with climate change.

Genetically diverse populations also vary in their resistance to pests and pathogens. For example, approximately one percent of beech trees (*Fagus grandifolia*) are naturally resistant to beech bark disease, a condition caused by a non-native scale insect introduced from Eurasia. These disease-resistant trees may carry a specific set of genes that could prove invaluable for future beech conservation and restoration efforts.

How to build genetic diversity in your landscape

Ninebark calligrapha beetle feeding on the leaves of its host, Atlantic ninebark (*Physocarpus opulifolius*).

The deep purple foliage of ninebark 'Diabolo'.

Minimize use of native plant cultivars
Cultivars—plant varieties cultivated by horticulturists—are often selected for a few narrow attributes such as growth rate, size, and flower color. Most of the native plants available in large nurseries are cultivars, which are usually propagated asexually by division, cuttings, and tissue culture. Although these practices retain the desired traits, the mass-production of cloned plants makes no contribution to genetic diversity. Selecting for certain desirable traits can also inadvertently fracture the fragile connections between plants, pollinators, and herbivores. The large, showy flowers of *Hydrangea* 'Annabelle', for example, are mostly sterile and cannot feed pollinators, and the dark foliage of *Physocarpus* 'Diabolo' may be less nutritious for herbivores than the straight species.

Seek out seed-grown native plants whenever possible
Instead of cultivars, we recommend that you purchase seed and seed-grown plants from your nearest native plant nursery; swap seeds with family and friends; and/or ethically collect seeds from right-of-ways, roadsides, public parks, and natural areas. If you have the time and patience, we also encourage you to participate in the full seed-to-seed life cycle of your garden by propagating seed-grown plants from your own landscape. Each handful of seed you collect will contain an original set of reshuffled genes from native plants known to grow well on your property.

Favor ecotypic seeds and plants when possible, but recognize their limitations
Ecotypic seeds—those collected from (and genetically suited to) a known location—are not commonly available for most native plants and ecoregions, so it's important to communicate demand to growers and support nurseries that do carry them. Locally grown ecotypic seeds are often the best option but are not necessarily a panacea. Rapid climate change and non-native plant, pest, and pathogen introductions compel us to consider seeds of native and 'near native' plant species sourced from warmer climes. Rather than rigidly pursuing plants from a specific ecotype, focus on building genetic diversity from a mix of local and regional seed sources, such as the Northeast *and* Mid-Atlantic, for plants suitable for your growing conditions.

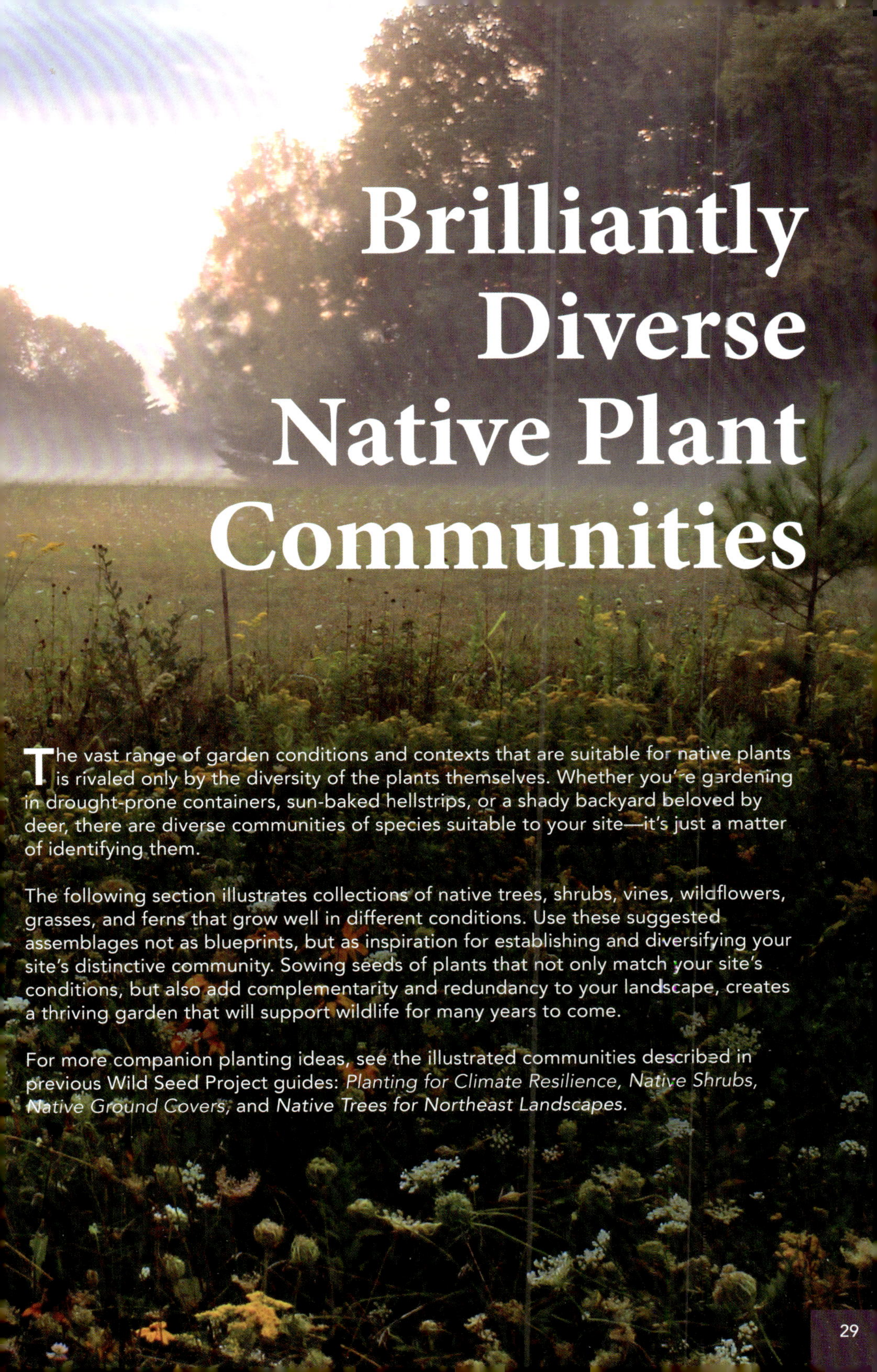

Brilliantly Diverse Native Plant Communities

The vast range of garden conditions and contexts that are suitable for native plants is rivaled only by the diversity of the plants themselves. Whether you're gardening in drought-prone containers, sun-baked hellstrips, or a shady backyard beloved by deer, there are diverse communities of species suitable to your site—it's just a matter of identifying them.

The following section illustrates collections of native trees, shrubs, vines, wildflowers, grasses, and ferns that grow well in different conditions. Use these suggested assemblages not as blueprints, but as inspiration for establishing and diversifying your site's distinctive community. Sowing seeds of plants that not only match your site's conditions, but also add complementarity and redundancy to your landscape, creates a thriving garden that will support wildlife for many years to come.

For more companion planting ideas, see the illustrated communities described in previous Wild Seed Project guides: *Planting for Climate Resilience, Native Shrubs, Native Ground Covers,* and *Native Trees for Northeast Landscapes.*

Sunlight Scavengers

Forest floor communities display complementarity across space and time, from the drifts of shade-tolerant ferns and summer herbs at the bases of trees to the staggered emergence of spring ephemerals before the canopy's summer closure.

COMMUNITY 1: MEDIUM TO WET **(SHOWN)** Yellow buckeye, leatherwood**, American spikenard*, northern lady fern, red baneberry, Virginia bluebells, large-flowered bellwort, Carolina spring beauty

COMMUNITY 2: MEDIUM TO DRY Scarlet oak, eastern wahoo, woodland sunflower, poke milkweed, downy skullcap, red columbine, goldenseal, bloodroot

Early Establishers

These disturbance-loving plants are quick to establish. They help stabilize soil, rebuild local food webs, and create invaluable early successional habitat in forest clearings and along roadsides and streambanks.

COMMUNITY 1: SUNNY, DRY **(SHOWN)** Gray birch, partridge pea, Kalm's brome sideoats grama, hoary vervain, pink corydalis, sundial lupine, narrow-leaved mountain mint

COMMUNITY 2: SUNNY, MEDIUM TO WET Tamarack, silky dogwood, swamp thistle, showy tick-trefoil, Canada wild rye, orange jewelweed, sensitive fern**, wild clematis*

*species not featured in this guide **species not featured here, but detailed in past guides

Acidic Soil Lovers

These resourceful scavengers thrive in the nutrient-limited, acidic soils common in the Northeast. As denizens of wet meadows, shrub thickets, and rich woods, many of these plants create wildlife-supporting ground covers, even beneath dense tree canopy.

COMMUNITY 1: SUN TO PART SHADE **(SHOWN)** Maleberry, pinxterbloom azalea, American fly honeysuckle**, bluejoint grass*, sheep laurel**, lowbush blueberry**, large cranberry, New York fern**

COMMUNITY 2: PART SHADE TO SHADE Sweet azalea, mountain laurel**, bog goldenrod, broad beech fern, wild ginger**, bunchberry**, partridgeberry

Container Dwellers

Many native plants thrive in containers, whether placed on a sunny balcony or a shady patio. These selections of plants can tolerate drying out between waterings. In exposed locations, you may need to protect planters with an insulating tarp through the winter.

COMMUNITY 1: SUNNY **(SHOWN)** Hoary vervain, common golden Alexanders*, beetberry, shortbeak sedge, strict blue-eyed grass, narrow-leaved sundrops, field pussytoes, flax-leaved stiff aster*

COMMUNITY 2: SHADY Blue lobelia, Small's beardtongue*, white snakeroot, red columbine, broad-leaved sedge, northern lady fern, partridgeberry

Herbivore Resisters

No plant is truly ignored by herbivores, but these species invest in extra physical and chemical defenses to dissuade browsing by deer, rabbits, and rodents. Defend more munchable wildflowers and vegetables by interspersing them with these resilient species.

COMMUNITY 1: SHADY, MEDIUM **(SHOWN)** Spicebush**, broad beech fern, Pennsylvania sedge**, common selfheal**, wild garlic**, orange jewelweed, red columbine, poke milkweed, goldenseal, white snakeroot

COMMUNITY 2: SUNNY, MEDIUM Inkberry holly**, Virginia rose**, fringed sedge, wild bee-balm, blue lobelia, wood betony, licorice goldenrod

Bold & Brilliant Competitors

Sets of splendid natives that are well-suited for replacing and crowding out aggressive, non-native species. Use caution when adding these beautiful but eager-to-spread plants in small landscapes or near early establishing and resource scavenging species.

COMMUNITY 1: SUNNY, MEDIUM TO WET **(SHOWN)** Silky dogwood, trumpet honeysuckle, swamp rose, New England aster, fringed sedge, green-headed coneflower, hollow Joe-Pye weed

COMMUNITY 1: SUNNY, DRY Staghorn sumac, Virginia rose**, switchgrass, foxglove beardtongue, wild bee-balm, common milkweed*, Canada milk vetch

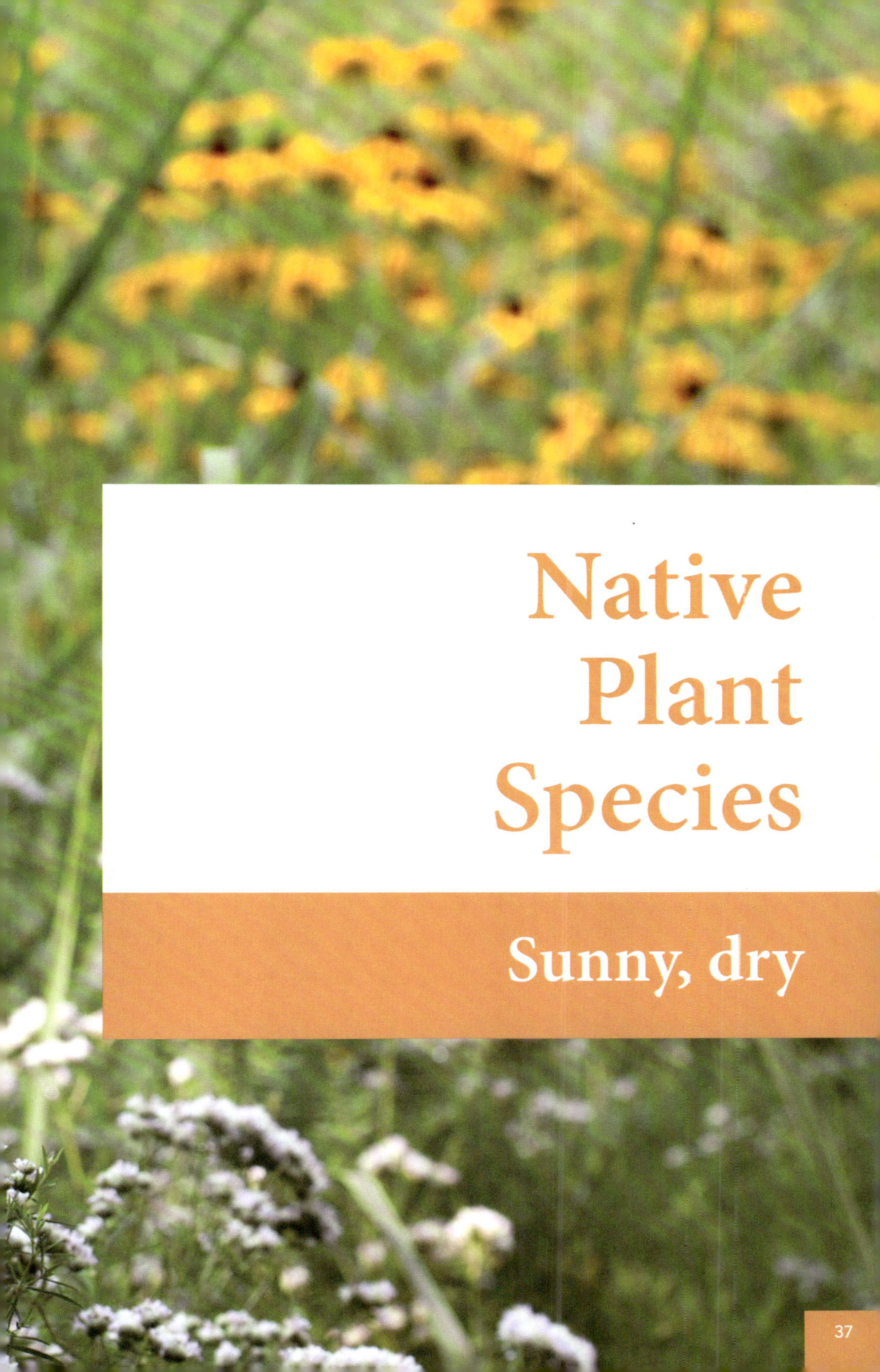

Native Plant Species

Sunny, dry

Field pussytoes

Antennaria neglecta

Soft and wooly from head to toe, field pussytoes form compact rosettes of gray-green leaves that slowly carpet rock gardens and struggling lawns.

Come mid- to late spring, clusters of fuzzy white flowers emerge, perched atop hairy stems that reach up to one foot tall. Unlike most members of the aster family, field pussytoes are dioecious, meaning each individual produces either staminate (pollen-bearing) or pistillate (seed-bearing) flowers. Borne on taller stems, the pistillate flowers give the plant its name, with clusters resembling miniature cats' feet, pawing the air. Staminate flowers are more rounded with yellow-brown stamens protruding from the center.

The plant serves as a larval host for the American lady butterfly and everlasting tebenna moth. Ravenous caterpillars may defoliate smaller populations by June, but this perennial reliably rebounds the following spring.

This hardy ground cover thrives in gravelly, shallow soils but also tolerates well-drained soils. It can withstand foot traffic and benefits from mowing to diminish nearby competitors—but avoid mowing when caterpillars are feeding during the summer.

ALSO TRY: Plantain-leaved pussytoes (*Antennaria plantaginifolia*)

LIGHT LEVEL: SHADE | **PART SHADE** | **SUN**

SOIL MOISTURE LEVEL: WET | **MEDIUM** | **DRY**

LIFESTYLE: EARLY ESTABLISHER | KEEN COMPETITOR | **RESOURCEFUL SCAVENGER**

HEIGHT: 1-4 IN

SPREAD: 6-12 IN

Strict blue-eyed grass

Sisyrinchium montanum

Sporting loose tufts of blue-gray leaves that emerge directly from the ground, this member of the Iris family looks deceptively like a grass when it first sprouts. Its cover is blown by late spring to early summer, however, when flattened stems emerge to reveal delicate sets of lustrous, star-like flowers.

The blue-violet blooms are marked with dark violet nectar guides that help direct pollinators—including green metallic bees and syrphid flies—towards the yellow-eyed center where the pollen-ladened stamens (and later, pollen-accepting stigmas) are located. The flowers close every evening to protect their pollen while the diurnal pollinators rest.

This adaptable perennial thrives in various settings, from rain gardens to sandy meadows. By growing in petite clumps that slowly spread via seed and thin rhizomes, blue-eyed grass is also well suited as edging along paths. Plant in sun to promote peak flowering.

ALSO TRY: Narrow-leaved blue-eyed grass (*Sisyrinchium angustifolium*)

LIGHT LEVEL: SHADE | PART SHADE | SUN

SOIL MOISTURE LEVEL: WET | MEDIUM | DRY

LIFESTYLE: EARLY ESTABLISHER | KEEN COMPETITOR | RESOURCEFUL SCAVENGER

HEIGHT: 5–12 IN

SPREAD: 6–8 IN

Wood betony

Pedicularis canadensis

This small statured perennial has fern-like foliage that emerges maroon, then fades to green as summer approaches. Wood betony has remarkably large flower-heads for such a short plant, each bearing dozens of yellow to reddish-purple tube-shaped flowers that often veer to one side, creating a pinwheel of blooms when viewed from above. Flowering April to May, wood betony offers much needed nectar to emerging queen bumble bees, including the at-risk golden northern (*Bombus fervidus*) and half-black (*B. vagans*) bumble bees.

Pedicularis spp. are also called louseworts, a name derived from an inconsistent set of folk legends that claim the plants rid (or perhaps cause?) lice infestations in livestock. Pure folklore, except that louseworts, like lice, are parasites! Hemi-parasites, to be precise, meaning wood betony can survive on its own just fine, but benefits from parasitizing the roots of nearby plants for nutrients. By reducing the height of neighboring hosts like grasses and asters, wood betony helps create open areas for less competitive, shade intolerant plants to grow.

Seed may lose viability if left to dry out, so sow fresh within a month of collecting.

ALSO TRY: Slender false foxglove (*Agalinis tenuifolia*)

LIGHT LEVEL: SHADE | **PART SHADE** | **SUN**

SOIL MOISTURE LEVEL: WET | **MEDIUM** | **DRY**

LIFESTYLE: EARLY ESTABLISHER | KEEN COMPETITOR | **RESOURCEFUL SCAVENGER**

HEIGHT: 4-12 IN

SPREAD: 6-12 IN

Bearing tall, densely packed spikes of creamy white flowers in the summer, Canada milk vetch attracts butterflies, bumble bees, and leafcutter bees, including the pollen specialist black-and-gray leafcutter bee. Like most legumes, this drought-tolerant perennial harbors beneficial bacteria in its roots that help supply nitrogen to the host plant along with the neighboring community. Milk vetches (*Astragalus* spp.) are a diverse genus that mostly hail from dry plains and mountains out west; Canada milk vetch is one of the few species native to the Northeast.

ALSO TRY: Wild goat's rue (*Tephrosia virginiana*)

Canada milk vetch

Astragalus canadensis

LIGHT LEVEL: SHADE · **PART SHADE** · **SUN**

SOIL MOISTURE LEVEL: WET · **MEDIUM** · **DRY**

LIFESTYLE: EARLY ESTABLISHER · **KEEN COMPETITOR** · RESOURCEFUL SCAVENGER

HEIGHT: 1-4 FT

SPREAD: 18-24 IN

This cheerful legume generously supports wildlife during its short annual lifecycle. The abundant flowers of the partridge pea are beloved by many bees as a mid-summer source of pollen; extrafloral nectaries at the base of leaf stalks attract butterflies, wasps, flies, lady-beetles, and ants. The foliage provides forage for sulphur butterfly larvae, including the little yellow, sleepy orange, and cloudless sulphur. Partridge pea enthusiastically self-seeds via brown pea-like pods that explosively split open in fall to expel the seeds within.

ALSO TRY: Wild sensitive pea (*Chamaecrista nictitans*)

Partridge pea

Chamaecrista fasciculata

LIGHT LEVEL: SHADE · **PART SHADE** · **SUN**

SOIL MOISTURE LEVEL: WET · **MEDIUM** · **DRY**

LIFESTYLE: **EARLY ESTABLISHER** · KEEN COMPETITOR · RESOURCEFUL SCAVENGER

HEIGHT: 6-36 IN

SPREAD: 6-12 IN

Sundial lupine

Lupinus perennis

This once wide-ranging perennial native to oak-savanna and sand barren habitats has become quite rare due to habitat loss and fire suppression. Palmate leaves and abundant light blue blooms (with occasional white to pinkish flower clusters) make this drought-tolerant and sand-loving species an attractive choice for a well-drained garden space.

The legume attracts myriad pollinators in spring to early summer and is the only larval host of the endangered Karner blue (pictured). This small butterfly has suffered from habitat loss and the introduction of big leaf lupine (*L. polyphyllus*), a non-native species that hybridizes with our native lupine to create offspring that are inedible to Karner blue caterpillars.

A member of the pea family, this species has a long tap root and is not a good candidate for transplanting. Grows well by seed that has been scarified and soaked.

LIGHT LEVEL: SHADE · **PART SHADE** · **SUN**

SOIL MOISTURE LEVEL: WET · MEDIUM · **DRY**

LIFESTYLE: EARLY ESTABLISHER · KEEN COMPETITOR · **RESOURCEFUL SCAVENGER**

HEIGHT 1-2 FT

SPREAD 8-12 IN

Narrow-leaved sundrops

Oenothera fruticosa ssp. glauca

Much shorter than its more familiar cousin, the common evening primrose (*O. biennis*), perennial narrow-leaved sundrops make an excellent addition to borders, rock gardens, meadow gardens, and hellstrips.

In late spring to early summer, deep red buds open up to reveal lively yellow blooms. Each four-petaled flower is short-lived, but the blooms carry on for months. True to their name, sundrop flowers open during the day and close by evening, unlike the nocturnal flowers of some relatives in the evening primrose family (Onagraceae).

Several butterfly species pollinate narrow-leaved sundrops, including skippers, as well as carpenter and leafcutter bees. The plant also supports the evening primrose sweat bee, a small black bee that specializes on the sticky, thread-like pollen from evening primroses. Leaves and distinctive club-shaped seed capsules serve as a critical food source for primrose moth larvae (pictured on evening primrose). Narrow-leaved sundrops readily self-seed, often with an assist from American goldfinches prying open the seed-filled capsules come fall.

ALSO TRY: Prairie sundrops (*Oenothera pilosella*), small sundrops (*O. perennis*)

LIGHT LEVEL				SOIL MOISTURE LEVEL				LIFESTYLE					
	SHADE	PART SHADE	SUN		WET	MEDIUM	DRY		EARLY ESTABLISHER	KEEN COMPETITOR	RESOURCEFUL SCAVENGER	HEIGHT	1–2 FT
												SPREAD	24–30 IN

Narrow-leaved mountain mint
Pycnanthemum tenuifolium

Forming bouquets of densely packed white flowers atop needle-like foliage, narrow-leaved mountain mint has a distinctly delicate appearance. Under this guise, however, is an extremely hardy perennial, capable of thriving in the driest and most sun-scorched spots of your garden. The long-blooming flowers attract bustling crowds of insects such as butterflies, beetles, plant bugs, bee flies, mydas flies, and thread-waisted wasps. Although not nearly as aggressive as cultivated mints, mountain mints may need to be divided to control their spread in smaller landscapes.

ALSO TRY: Virginia mountain mint (*Pycnanthemum virginianum*)

LIGHT LEVEL: SHADE | PART SHADE | SUN

SOIL MOISTURE LEVEL: WET | MEDIUM | DRY

LIFESTYLE: EARLY ESTABLISHER | KEEN COMPETITOR | RESOURCEFUL SCAVENGER

HEIGHT: 2-3 FT

SPREAD: 1-3 FT

Wild bee-balm
Monarda fistulosa

Wild bee-balm is a versatile must-have perennial for any native garden. The characteristic crown of lavender flowers bloom at the height of summer and attract long-tongued bees, butterflies, and clearwing moths. Though better known for flocking to scarlet bee-balm, hummingbirds also relish the nectar of wild bee-balm. The oregano-scented foliage feeds larvae of the hermit sphinx and raspberry pyrausta moths, and also makes a pleasant tea. It's one of the easiest wildflowers to sow, as the seeds require no cold period to germinate!

ALSO TRY: Bradbury's bee-balm (*Monarda bradburiana*)

LIGHT LEVEL: SHADE | PART SHADE | SUN

SOIL MOISTURE LEVEL: WET | MEDIUM | DRY

LIFESTYLE: EARLY ESTABLISHER | KEEN COMPETITOR | RESOURCEFUL SCAVENGER

HEIGHT: 2-4 FT

SPREAD: 12-18 IN

Pink corydalis

Capnoides sempervirens

An eccentric member of the poppy family, this biennial produces a rosette of lacey, greenish-blue leaves its first year, followed by a branching flowering stem the next spring. Curious clusters of pink and yellow tubular flowers bloom and dangle off the stem between May and September.

Bumble bees and other long-tongued bees push their heads between the outer and inner petals to reach the nectar stored high up in the flower's blunt spur. The blooms give way to long, bean-like pods that peel open to reveal small black seeds. Each seed has a fleshy attachment called an elaiosome that entices ants to stash them away in their nests, helping to disperse the seeds in the process. Once lost to the soil, seeds can remain viable for decades as they wait for an opportune disturbance to sprout.

A weak competitor that is easily lost among nearby vegetation, pink corydalis is best appreciated when planted along walkways, between pavers, or in rock gardens.

ALSO TRY: Yellow corydalis (*Corydalis flavula*)

LIGHT LEVEL: SHADE · PART SHADE · SUN

SOIL MOISTURE LEVEL: WET · MEDIUM · DRY

LIFESTYLE: EARLY ESTABLISHER · KEEN COMPETITOR · RESOURCEFUL SCAVENGER

HEIGHT: 6-36 IN

SPREAD: 6-24 IN

Foxglove beardtongue

Penstemon digitalis

Adorned with panicles of white to pale pink tubular flowers that bloom from early- to mid-summer, foxglove beardtongue helps bridge the gap between fading spring flowers and pending mid-summer blooms.

Each flower tube is adorned with several pink-purple striped nectar guides that advertise *"free nectar this way!"* to passing bumble bees. As these stocky pollinators squeeze their way inside a bloom, curved stamens drop pollen on their backs out of the bee's reach yet well-positioned to stick to the stigma of the next flower the bee visits. The nectar-filled blooms are also popular among solitary bees, butterflies, sphinx moths, and hummingbirds.

The name 'beardtongue' references the sterile stamen located at the bottom of the flower tube, which is covered in sparse yellow hairs. These hairs may nudge the bee to go further into the flower and may help catch dropped pollen and re-deposit it on the next visitor.

The attractive foliage matures quickly in the spring and tends to escape predation by deer.

ALSO TRY: Northeastern beardtongue (*Penstemon hirsutus*)

LIGHT LEVEL: SHADE · **PART SHADE** · **SUN**

SOIL MOISTURE LEVEL: WET · **MEDIUM** · **DRY**

LIFESTYLE: **EARLY ESTABLISHER** · KEEN COMPETITOR · RESOURCEFUL SCAVENGER

HEIGHT: 2-4 FT

SPREAD: 12-18 IN

Hoary vervain

Verbena stricta

True to its name, the gray-green leaves and square stems of hoary vervain are heavily covered with long white hairs. The exceptional fuzziness helps deter deer, but does not dissuade many insect herbivores, including red-legged grasshoppers and fine-lined sallow and verbena moth caterpillars.

This vigorous, clump-forming wildflower forms columns of densely-packed, bright violet flowers that bloom from the bottom up for four to six weeks in July and August. Flowers are larger than those of its cousin, the moisture-loving blue vervain (*V. hastata*).

Hoary vervain is not native to the Northeast, but rather originates from the Midwest, where some consider it a pasture weed. The short-lived perennial thrives in sandy and gravelly soils, but adapts to a wider range of conditions so long as competition remains minimal.

The tall fruit-bearing spikes persist well into the winter, providing visual interest and delectable seeds for cardinals, juncos, and field sparrows.

ALSO TRY: Smooth blue aster (*Symphyotrichum laeve*)

LIGHT LEVEL: SHADE, PART SHADE, **SUN**

SOIL MOISTURE LEVEL: WET, MEDIUM, **DRY**

LIFESTYLE: **EARLY ESTABLISHER**, KEEN COMPETITOR, RESOURCEFUL SCAVENGER

HEIGHT: 2–4 FT

SPREAD: 18–24 IN

Sideoats grama

Bouteloua curtipendula

This medium-sized perennial grass earned its "tough as boots" reputation by helping to stabilize soils during the Dust Bowl. The plant's resilience stems from being a warm-season grass that is adapted to grow best during the height of summer. Roughly half of all grasses belong to this group—including tropical species like maize and sugarcane—with members capable of a special form of photosynthesis that excels under the hot, dry conditions of peak summer.

Sideoats grama has distinctive, mid-summer flowers with purplish, oat-like floral spikes that hang like ornaments from a zigzagging stem. Look closer and find that the floral spikes are adorned with showy red-orange stamens and delicate, feather-like white stigmas. By fall, the spikes turn tan while the foliage turns golden brown with hues of purple and red.

Although its range stretches from southern Canada to Argentina, sideoats grama is quite rare in the Northeast. This might be due to its preference for moderately alkaline soils, so consider planting this grass near asphalt or concrete where soil pH is often elevated.

ALSO TRY: Purple love grass (*Eragrostis spectabilis*)

LIGHT LEVEL: SHADE · **PART SHADE** · **SUN**

SOIL MOISTURE LEVEL: WET · **MEDIUM** · **DRY**

LIFESTYLE: **EARLY ESTABLISHER** · KEEN COMPETITOR · **RESOURCEFUL SCAVENGER**

HEIGHT: 1-3 FT

SPREAD: 1-2 FT

Kalm's brome

Bromus kalmii

Also known as prairie brome, this short-lived perennial grass dons attractive silky spikelets that hang gracefully off an arching stem. The wind-pollinated flowering spikelets grow light green to purple-gray, urning tan as the fruit matures.

This cool-season grass finishes growing by early summer, when it then becomes overtopped by nearby heat-loving plants. Naturally found on outcrops and in sandy woodland clearings, Kalm's brome is endangered in Maine and New Hampshire, where it reaches the northern limit of its range.

ALSO TRY: Curly oat grass (*Danthonia spicata*)

LIGHT LEVEL: SHADE, **PART SHADE**, **SUN**

SOIL MOISTURE LEVEL: WET, **MEDIUM**, **DRY**

LIFESTYLE: **EARLY ESTABLISHER**, KEEN COMPETITOR, RESOURCEFUL SCAVENGER

HEIGHT: 2-3 FT

SPREAD: 12-18 IN

Switchgrass

Panicum virgatum

This extremely versatile, perennial warm-season grass can grow in almost any soil, and can endure stress from drought, flooding, and road salt.

Switchgrass develops large airy clusters of flowers comprised of green to purple spikelets suspended from wiry stems. The robust clumps of foliage turn golden brown in fall. Protect vital winter cover for wildlife by waiting until April to prune back.

An excellent alternative to non-native silver grasses (*Miscanthus* spp.) that belong to several state invasive plant lists. Makes an excellent screen.

ALSO TRY: Purpletop tridens (*Tridens flavus*)

LIGHT LEVEL: SHADE, PART SHADE, **SUN**

SOIL MOISTURE LEVEL: **WET**, **MEDIUM**, **DRY**

LIFESTYLE: EARLY ESTABLISHER, **KEEN COMPETITOR**, RESOURCEFUL SCAVENGER

HEIGHT: 3-6 FT

SPREAD: 2-4 FT

Staghorn sumac

Rhus hirta

Staghorn sumac is an underappreciated yet remarkably attractive native shrub with distinctive clusters of bright red fuzzy fruit.

Our largest native sumac, this common roadside plant has substantial ecological value. Short-tongued bees, flies, ants, beetles, and mason wasps seek out the green-yellow flowers in early- to mid-summer. The leaves provide food for sumac flea beetles and caterpillars of the red-banded hairstreak butterfly and showy emerald moth. Many birds rely on the fuzzy red fruit for much-needed forage during winter, including wild turkeys, northern flickers, cedar waxwings, chickadees, and evening grosbeaks (pictured). The suckering growth habit also provides important wildlife cover; carpenter bees may use the soft pith of stems for nesting sites.

Excellent at stabilizing slopes, staghorn sumac spreads vigorously, so this competitive shrub is not suitable for smaller landscapes. New shoots are intolerant of mowing, so regular cutting can manage spread.

Common name references the dense, brown hairs that cover the upper branches, resembling deer antlers in velvet.

ALSO TRY: Smooth sumac (*Rhus glabra*)

LIGHT LEVEL: SHADE · PART SHADE · SUN

SOIL MOISTURE LEVEL: WET · MEDIUM · DRY

LIFESTYLE: EARLY ESTABLISHER · KEEN COMPETITOR · RESOURCEFUL SCAVENGER

HEIGHT: 10–25 FT

SPREAD: 10–25 FT

Gray birch

Betula populifolia

Among the hardiest of birches, this fast-growing yet short-lived tree grows as a single- or multi-stemmed form with a narrow pyramidal crown. Mature trees have grayish-white bark that does not peel like paper birch bark, but still provides year-round interest.

Like all birches, gray birch produces separate staminate (pictured) and pistillate flower spikes (catkins) that emerge on the same tree in early spring before leaf-out. Pistillate catkins droop as they mature, producing cone-like clusters full of wind-dispersed seeds.

All parts of this native tree provide food for wildlife, laying the foundation of local food webs. The glossy triangular leaves feed larvae of the mourning cloak, Compton tortoiseshell, and eastern tiger swallowtail butterflies, as well as several species of leaf-mining sawflies. The winged seeds provide food for pine siskins and black-capped chickadees, and the sweet sap feeds yellow-bellied sapsuckers. Hares, porcupines, and beavers eat the bark and twigs.

This scrappy species tolerates soil compaction, road salt, and most soil types; well-suited for many urban settings.

ALSO TRY: Quaking aspen (*Populus tremuloides*); pin cherry (*Prunus pensylvanica*)

LIGHT LEVEL: SHADE · **PART SHADE** · **SUN**

SOIL MOISTURE LEVEL: WET · **MEDIUM** · **DRY**

LIFESTYLE: **EARLY ESTABLISHER** · KEEN COMPETITOR · RESOURCEFUL SCAVENGER

HEIGHT: 20–40 FT

SPREAD: 10–20 FT

Native Plant Species

Sunny, medium-to-wet

Beetberry

Chenopodium capitatum

Also called strawberry spinach, this unusual annual appeals to people and wildlife alike. Closely related to lambsquarters, beetberry belongs to the eclectic amaranth family. Other members include beets, spinach, and quinoa, as well as our native salt-tolerant glassworts.

Summer blooms contain numerous light green petal-less flowers that grow tightly packed in ball-shaped clusters that hug the stem. Once wind-pollinated, bright red and fleshy fruit clusters develop, resembling berries from afar.

Although dismissed as a weed by many gardeners, beetberry can be a valuable food source for insects and birds. It serves as a larval host for the common sootywing skipper (pictured), as well as the virgin tiger and chenopodium scythris moths. The plentiful seeds are eaten by songbirds, especially sparrows.

Beetberry leaves can be eaten like spinach (raw or cooked) and the mild fruit is rich in betalains, the same pigment found in beets. May not transplant well, so direct sowing in the spring (or late fall) is recommended.

LIGHT LEVEL: SHADE | **PART SHADE** | **SUN**

SOIL MOISTURE LEVEL: WET | **MEDIUM** | DRY

LIFESTYLE: **EARLY ESTABLISHER** | KEEN COMPETITOR | RESOURCEFUL SCAVENGER

HEIGHT: 8-24 IN

SPREAD: 1-2 FT

Showy tick-trefoil

Desmodium canadense

Blooming in midsummer, this tall perennial legume grows spikes of densely-packed pink and violet pea-like flowers that attract bumble bees, leaf-cutter bees, and long-horned bees. The nectar-less blooms hold the pollen-bearing stamens within the keel petals until a heavy-enough pollinator visits and trips their release, flinging a cloud of pollen onto the unsuspecting visitor.

The trifoliate leaves host several butterfly and moth species, including the eastern tailed blue, gray hairstreak, northern cloudywing skipper, and tentiform bean leafminer moth. Like many legumes, showy tick-trefoil also attracts mammalian herbivores—including deer, rabbits, and groundhogs—so fencing may be needed.

Hook-like hairs cover the fruits and act like Velcro to attach to the fur (or pants) of animals. Avoid planting tick-trefoils near sidewalks where the seeds from sprawling plants may cling to unwitting passersby.

Prior to sowing, remove hulls from the kidney-shaped seeds or scarify the unhulled seeds with coarse sandpaper.

ALSO TRY: Panicled tick-trefoil (*Desmodium paniculatum*)

LIGHT LEVEL: SHADE · **PART SHADE** · **SUN**

SOIL MOISTURE LEVEL: WET · **MEDIUM** · DRY

LIFESTYLE: EARLY ESTABLISHER · **KEEN COMPETITOR** · RESOURCEFUL SCAVENGER

HEIGHT: 3-5 FT

SPREAD: 1-2 FT

Swamp thistle

Cirsium muticum

Often unjustly maligned as prickly noxious weeds, native thistles deserve wider appreciation and adoption. Unlike the non-native Canada thistle—an aggressive perennial that does have sharp prickles—swamp thistle is a considerably less prickly biennial that spreads slowly by seed. Its stately structure and large striking blooms attract droves of pollinators and add beauty to any garden.

As a biennial, swamp thistle lives a short but sweet life. It forms a rosette of basal leaves in its first year, followed by a tall stem with vibrant pinkish-purple flower heads in its second year. Each flower head contains numerous nectar-filled florets that are among the most attractive flowers to butterflies and bees.

Frequently visited by monarchs, swallowtails, fritillaries, bumble bees, and the thistle long-horned bee—a pollen specialist that is listed as imperiled in Vermont. American goldfinches, juncos, sparrows, and indigo buntings all relish the seed.

ALSO TRY: Field thistle (*Cirsium discolor*)

LIGHT LEVEL: SHADE · PART SHADE · SUN

SOIL MOISTURE LEVEL: WET · MEDIUM · DRY

LIFESTYLE: EARLY ESTABLISHER · KEEN COMPETITOR · RESOURCEFUL SCAVENGER

HEIGHT: 3–7 FT

SPREAD: 1–2 FT

Licorice goldenrod

Solidago odora

Contrary to popular belief, most goldenrod species are non-aggressive and coexist well alongside other plants. Good thing, too, as goldenrods lay the foundations of local food webs. Late nectar-rich blooms help migrating monarchs refuel and queen bumble bees build up winter fat reserves; dense flowers feed more pollen specialist bee species than any other native plant; and the plentiful foliage hosts more butterfly and moth species than any other wildflower.

Licorice goldenrod provides all these benefits and more. Anise-scented leaves deter deer.

ALSO TRY: Showy goldenrod (*Solidago speciosa*)

LIGHT LEVEL: SHADE · **PART SHADE** · **SUN**

SOIL MOISTURE LEVEL: WET · **MEDIUM** · **DRY**

LIFESTYLE: EARLY ESTABLISHER · **KEEN COMPETITOR** · RESOURCEFUL SCAVENGER

HEIGHT: 2–4 FT

SPREAD: 1–2 FT

New England aster

Symphyotrichum novae-angliae

This vibrant perennial blooms alongside goldenrod between August and November, offering up a dependably beautiful pairing that marks the end of summer. Amongst our showiest of native aster species, the deep purple to light pink flowers are large for an aster. Many pollinators and herbivores rely on this late-bloomer for sustenance, including the flower-eating larvae of the brown-hooded owlet and wavy-lined emerald moths.

Plant this eager self-seeder with caution in small landscapes. Prune back in June to achieve bushier growth.

ALSO TRY: Purple-stemmed aster (*Symphyotrichum puniceum*)

LIGHT LEVEL: SHADE · **PART SHADE** · **SUN**

SOIL MOISTURE LEVEL: **WET** · **MEDIUM** · DRY

LIFESTYLE: **EARLY ESTABLISHER** · **KEEN COMPETITOR** · RESOURCEFUL SCAVENGER

HEIGHT: 2–5 FT

SPREAD: 2–3 FT

Green-headed coneflower

Rudbeckia laciniata

Towering overhead, this woodland wildflower is distinctive among *Rudbeckia* spp. for its green flower centers and drooping yellow ray florets that bloom from July to October. Also known as cutleaf coneflower for its attractive lobed leaves.

Prefers part-shade but will grow in full sun with enough moisture. Plant near other tall plants for support and to offset lankiness.

Can spread aggressively by rhizomes. Select the straight species over the popular cultivar 'Golden Glow' (*R. laciniata* 'Hortensia'), whose double flowerheads offer little to pollinators.

ALSO TRY: Brown-eyed coneflower (*Rudbeckia triloba*)

LIGHT LEVEL: SHADE · **PART SHADE** · **SUN**

SOIL MOISTURE LEVEL: WET · **MEDIUM** · DRY

LIFESTYLE: EARLY ESTABLISHER · **KEEN COMPETITOR** · RESOURCEFUL SCAVENGER

HEIGHT 3-7 FT

SPREAD 2-4 FT

Hollow Joe-Pye weed

Eutrochium fistulosum

The largest of the Joe-Pye weeds, this grand perennial puts on a bold late-summer display of pinkish-purple blooms arranged in dome-like clusters. Below the flowers are large leaves, up to 1′ long, arranged around a hollow stem.

Effective at creating structure in the garden, hollow Joe-Pye weed is also highly adaptable and tolerates heat, temporary flooding, and diverse soil types.

Eutrochium spp. are commonly misidentified in the nursery trade, so seek out seed and plants from reputable native plant nurseries.

ALSO TRY: Spotted Joe-Pye weed (*Eutrochium maculatum*)

LIGHT LEVEL: SHADE · **PART SHADE** · **SUN**

SOIL MOISTURE LEVEL: **WET** · **MEDIUM** · DRY

LIFESTYLE: EARLY ESTABLISHER · **KEEN COMPETITOR** · RESOURCEFUL SCAVENGER

HEIGHT 3-8 FT

SPREAD 3-4 FT

Canada wild rye

Elymus canadensis

This perennial cool-season grass is admired for its large nodding seed heads that sway gracefully in the summer breeze. Summer foliage varies from green to blue-green and fades to a bleached tan by fall. The persistent seed heads provide excellent winter interest.

Canada wild rye is a short-lived perennial that rapidly establishes on a range of soils. A non-aggressive grass that spreads by self-seeding rather than rhizomes, Canada wild rye usually fades over time as longer-lived perennials become established. These traits make it an excellent native cover crop to stabilize soil and suppress weeds.

Although its presence on the landscape may be fleeting, this grass provides much-needed winter cover for wildlife and good nesting habitat for songbirds. The leaves are eaten by various leafhoppers and caterpillars of the false wainscot moth.

ALSO TRY: Virginia wild rye (*Elymus virginicus*)

LIGHT LEVEL: SHADE | PART SHADE | SUN

SOIL MOISTURE LEVEL: WET | MEDIUM | DRY

LIFESTYLE: EARLY ESTABLISHER | KEEN COMPETITOR | RESOURCEFUL SCAVENGER

HEIGHT: 3-5 FT

SPREAD: 2-3 FT

Shortbeak sedge
Carex brevior

Largely underappreciated, sedges deserve a spot in every garden. These grass-like perennials are elegant, versatile, and low-maintenance. Although most ubiquitous in wetlands, hundreds of native *Carex* spp. grow in the Northeast, meaning there is a sedge for essentially any growing condition.

Shortbeak sedge is a short, clump-forming species with a mounded profile. Commonly found in disturbed areas with sandy or rocky soil, this sedge also tolerates moist garden soils. Effective as a ground cover to stabilize soil and suppress weeds.

ALSO TRY: Pointed broom sedge (*Carex scoparia*)

LIGHT LEVEL: SHADE, PART SHADE, SUN

SOIL MOISTURE LEVEL: WET, MEDIUM, DRY

LIFESTYLE: EARLY ESTABLISHER, KEEN COMPETITOR, RESOURCEFUL SCAVENGER

HEIGHT: 1-3 FT

SPREAD: 6-10 IN

Fringed sedge
Carex crinita

A large distinctive sedge that produces delicately drooping flowering spikes above blue-green foliage. Fruit follows by late spring, persisting well into fall. Like many sedges, fringed sedge hosts several species of satyrid butterfly, skipper, and owlet moth caterpillars. The leaves also feed sedge grass-hoppers, meadow katydids, reed beetles, and billbug weevils.

Clumps spread slowly, making this an effective mass planting, or a compatible member of a diverse meadow, rain garden, or border. This versatile sedge will thrive most anywhere with moisture.

ALSO TRY: Hayden's sedge (*Carex haydenii*)

LIGHT LEVEL: SHADE, PART SHADE, SUN

SOIL MOISTURE LEVEL: WET, MEDIUM, DRY

LIFESTYLE: EARLY ESTABLISHER, KEEN COMPETITOR, RESOURCEFUL SCAVENGER

HEIGHT: 2-4 FT

SPREAD: 1-2 FT

Trumpet honeysuckle

Lonicera sempervirens

Few plants have blooms as prolific and long-lasting as trumpet honeysuckle. Arranged in whorls around the tips of stems, the showstopping red flowers bloom profusely in May, then sporadically until fall. The nectar-filled, tube-shaped flowers are primarily pollinated by hummingbirds but also attract numerous butterflies and other long-tongued insects. Many songbirds relish the orange-red berries, including purple finches, hermit thrushes, and catbirds.

A twining perennial vine, trumpet honeysuckle can be trained up a trellis, arbor, or fence, or simply left to scramble down a bank. It also makes a great potted plant. The vine's vigorous growth benefits from occasional pruning; trim back after the first spring flush of flowers to retain next year's blooms.

Most large nurseries sell genetically uniform cultivars (e.g., 'Major Wheeler,' 'John Clayton'), so seek out the straight species from native plant nurseries.

ALSO TRY: Wild honeysuckle (*Lonicera dioica*)

LIGHT LEVEL: SHADE · PART SHADE · SUN

SOIL MOISTURE LEVEL: WET · MEDIUM · DRY

LIFESTYLE: EARLY ESTABLISHER · KEEN COMPETITOR · RESOURCEFUL SCAVENGER

HEIGHT: 4–15 FT

SPREAD: 4–8 FT

Large cranberry

Vaccinium macrocarpon

The forebear of cultivated cranberries, large cranberry is a bog-loving perennial ground cover that forms dense mats of glossy evergreen foliage. Nodding flowers emerge by late spring, distinguished by their pinkish-white petals that curl back like a lily. The plant derives its name from "craneberry," a moniker based on the loose resemblance of its nodding flowers to the head of a crane.

Although not bred for flavor like cultivated varieties, wild-type cranberries are edible just the same, and become deliciously sweet and tart when cooked. The bright red berries ripen in early autumn and often persist through winter if not devoured by birds and small mammals.

Large cranberry and its cousin, small cranberry (*V. oxycoccus*), are the only larval host plants for the bog copper butterfly. Unfortunately, insecticides often exclude these butterflies from commercial bogs.

Although well-suited for boggy areas, large cranberry can also thrive in gardens with consistently moist, well-drained, and acidic (pH 4.0 – 5.2) soils.

ALSO TRY: Mountain cranberry (*Vaccinium vitis-idaea* ssp. *minus*)

LIGHT LEVEL: SHADE · PART SHADE · **SUN**

SOIL MOISTURE LEVEL: **WET** · MEDIUM · DRY

LIFESTYLE: EARLY ESTABLISHER · KEEN COMPETITOR · **RESOURCEFUL SCAVENGER**

HEIGHT: 1-6 IN

SPREAD: 18-36 IN

Swamp rose

Rosa palustris

Swamp rose makes a beautifully fragrant addition to any border hedge, rain garden, or pond margin. This upright deciduous shrub has gracefully arching branches armed with stout, downwardly curved prickles. Leaves turn an attractive red-burgundy in the fall.

In early summer, swamp rose is covered in a profusion of sweetly-scented blooms that last six to eight weeks. The single-petaled roses are light pink, up to 3" across, and are often pink or orange-red in the center of the bloom. The nectarless flowers attract all kinds of pollen-consuming insects, including bumble bees, sweat bees, syrphid flies, and slender longhorn and tumbling flower beetles (pictured). The leaves are beloved by larvae of the stinging rose moth and various sawflies, leaf rolling weevils, and rose leafhoppers.

This is one of the only native roses that thrives in wet, poorly-drained soils. Roses can be semi-aggressive, so prune as needed in the late winter. Seeds require a double dormancy, so expect germination two years after fall sowing.

ALSO TRY: Smooth rose (*Rosa blanda*)

LIGHT LEVEL: SHADE | PART SHADE | SUN

SOIL MOISTURE LEVEL: WET | MEDIUM | DRY

LIFESTYLE: EARLY ESTABLISHER | KEEN COMPETITOR | RESOURCEFUL SCAVENGER

HEIGHT: 3-5 FT

SPREAD: 2-4 FT

Silky dogwood

Swida amomum

This medium-sized shrub has an open, rounded form and develops pleasing reddish-purple foliage in the fall. Tolerates deeper shade than many other dogwoods, but twigs and branches will only turn a beautiful deep red if exposed to full sun. This shrub appreciates a moisture-retentive layer of wood or leaf mulch over its roots, especially when planted in full sun.

Flowers from May to June. Like other dogwoods, blooms are flat-topped clusters that contain numerous four-petaled white flowers that attract an array of pollinators, including beetles, butterflies, wasps, bumble bees, and several species of pollen specialist, dogwood mining bees.

After the flowers fade, drooping clusters of fruit develop and change from white to an eye-catching silvery blue once ripe. Fruiting coincides with fall bird migration, helping to sustain many songbird species as they travel south. Lest they go to waste, leftover fruits are polished off by ground-foraging wild turkeys, small mammals, and even painted turtles!

ALSO TRY: Gray dogwood (*Swida racemosa*); red-osier dogwood (*S. sericea*)

LIGHT LEVEL: SHADE | PART SHADE | SUN

SOIL MOISTURE LEVEL: WET | MEDIUM | DRY

LIFESTYLE: EARLY ESTABLISHER | KEEN COMPETITOR | RESOURCEFUL SCAVENGER

HEIGHT: 6-12 FT

SPREAD: 4-8 FT

Pinxterbloom azalea

Rhododendron periclymenoides

Few spring blooms are as highly-anticipated as the exuberant displays of rhododendrons and azaleas. This deciduous understory shrub is one of the first native azaleas to flower in the spring. Pinxterbloom bears pink to white masses of delicately fragrant, tube-shaped flowers that attract swallowtail butterflies, bees, and hummingbirds.

Typical of members of the heath (Ericaceae) family, pinxterbloom azalea prefers moist but well-draining acidic soil. Tolerates moderately dry sandy or rocky substrates far more than slow-draining clay soil. Strong afternoon sun can scorch the leaves.

ALSO TRY: Early azalea (*Rhododendron prinophyllum*)

LIGHT LEVEL: SHADE · **PART SHADE** · **SUN**

SOIL MOISTURE LEVEL: WET · **MEDIUM** · DRY

LIFESTYLE: EARLY ESTABLISHER · KEEN COMPETITOR · **RESOURCEFUL SCAVENGER**

HEIGHT: 3-8 FT

SPREAD: 4-6 FT

Maleberry

Lyonia ligustrina

This single- to multi-stemmed, deciduous shrub has glossy green leaves that turn a delightful orange-red in the fall.

From May to June, stems terminate in bunches of urn-shaped white flowers that attract maleberry mining and blunt-horned bees—highly specialized species that only collect pollen from *Lyonia* spp. Flowers mature into small, dry capsules that split open upon ripening in early fall. Capsules persist year-round, slowly "salt-shaking" their seeds into the wind.

Often found between wetlands and upland shrub thickets, this ericaceous shrub grows well in any acidic, medium-draining soil.

ALSO TRY: Highbush blueberry (*Vaccinium corymbosum*)

LIGHT LEVEL: SHADE · **PART SHADE** · SUN

SOIL MOISTURE LEVEL: **WET** · MEDIUM · DRY

LIFESTYLE: EARLY ESTABLISHER · KEEN COMPETITOR · **RESOURCEFUL SCAVENGER**

HEIGHT: 6-12 FT

SPREAD: 6-12 FT

Silky willow

Salix sericea

The humble willow is one of the most underappreciated—if not unnoticed—native plants available to gardeners. Willows are tough as nails and, ecologically speaking, incredibly valuable; they form the foundation of local food webs and create vital habitat for wildlife. With almost thirty willow species native to the Northeast, options of all sizes and soil tolerances exist here.

Silky willow is a moisture-loving, medium-sized species with distinctive silvery-green undersides to its leaves. The early spring flowers are a vital source of nectar and pollen for ground-nesting bees, including the specialist red-tailed mining bee (pictured). Silky willow is a larval host for the Acadian hairstreak butterfly (pictured).

Plant far from pavement, sewage lines, and septic fields, as the vigorous shallow roots can cause damage. Herbivores love the new tender growth on willows, so protect first-year plantings with tall perimeter fencing. Once established, periodic heavy pruning in the winter will help control spread.

ALSO TRY: Meadow willow (*Salix petiolaris*)

LIGHT LEVEL: SHADE | PART SHADE | SUN

SOIL MOISTURE LEVEL: WET | MEDIUM | DRY

LIFESTYLE: EARLY ESTABLISHER | KEEN COMPETITOR | RESOURCEFUL SCAVENGER

HEIGHT: 10–12 FT

SPREAD: 8–12 FT

Tamarack

Larix laricina

Also called eastern larch, tamarack is the only deciduous conifer native to the Northeast. This medium to large tree has an open pyramidal shape and horizontal branches adorned with tight clusters of remarkably soft needles. In the fall, after many hardwoods have already lost their leaves, the green foliage turns a gorgeous golden yellow before dropping.

Often occurring as long-lived but stunted trees in open bogs and boreal swamps, tamarack is accustomed to very cold climates. Under cultivation, the tree is fast-growing and adaptable to a range of soils, from moist sand to mucky clay. As conifers go, tamarack casts a light shade compatible with understory plantings.

Pollen and seed cones grow on separate branches of the same tree (monoecious). Small, egg-shaped cones mature from a rosy pink to brown and often remain on the tree for several years, feeding red squirrels and boreal birds such as red crossbills and pine siskins. Tamarack is a larval host for the Columbia silkmoth and poecila sphinx moth.

ALSO TRY: Balsam fir (*Abies balsamea*)

LIGHT LEVEL: SHADE, PART SHADE, SUN

SOIL MOISTURE LEVEL: WET, MEDIUM, DRY

LIFESTYLE: EARLY ESTABLISHER, KEEN COMPETITOR, RESOURCEFUL SCAVENGER

HEIGHT: 30–60 FT

SPREAD: 10–20 FT

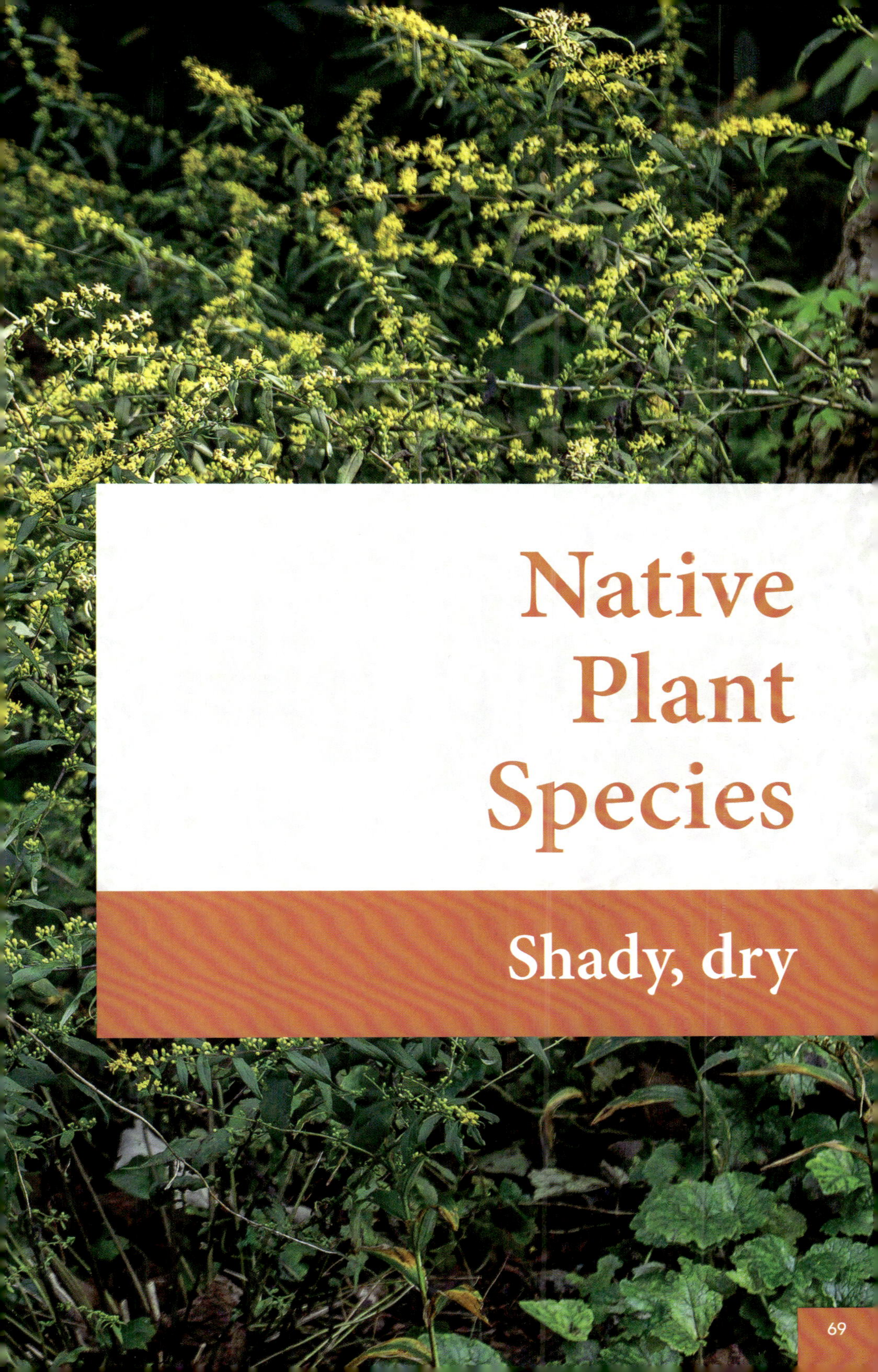

Native Plant Species

Shady, dry

Patridgeberry

Mitchella repens

The small, rounded leaves of partridgeberry carpets forest floors with deep evergreen foliage. Tiny spring-blooming white flowers provide an important food source for woodland pollinators. These fragrant blooms give way to bright red berries that can persist into winter if small mammals or birds such as wild turkeys and quail don't get to them first.

Usually found in shady dry to mesic forests throughout eastern North America, this species is common to find while on a woodland stroll, but not often in garden centers. This mildly drought tolerant and deer resistant species could be a good option for a shade garden if given the time and patience to establish. Though partridgeberry can be propagated by seed, it tends to be slow to establish and slow to spread.

ALSO TRY: Common wintergreen (*Gaultheria procumbens*)

LIGHT LEVEL: SHADE, PART SHADE, SUN

SOIL MOISTURE LEVEL: WET, MEDIUM, DRY

LIFESTYLE: EARLY ESTABLISHER, KEEN COMPETITOR, RESOURCEFUL SCAVENGER

HEIGHT: 1–2 IN

SPREAD: 10–14 IN

Bloodroot

Sanguinaria canadensis

A true harbinger of spring, this ephemeral blooms for about two weeks in March and April, though each fleeting flower lasts for only a day or two. Blooms are large and bright white with numerous yellow stamens. A single deeply-scalloped leaf envelops the flowering stalk and continues to unfurl and expand long after the bloom is spent. The plants vanish by late summer, lying dormant underground until the following spring.

Like many woodland wildflowers, bloodroot relies not on wind for seed dispersal but, instead, on ants. An oily attachment on the seeds, called an elaiosome, offers ants a quick meal in return for a free ride into their germination-friendly nest.

The sterile double flower cultivars (e.g., 'Multiplex') are touted for their longer blooms, a feat made possible by depriving early spring pollinators of much-needed pollen. When seeking out the straight species, only purchase plants from reputable nurseries to ensure they have not been collected from the wild.

ALSO TRY: Sharp-lobed hepatica (*Anemone acutiloba*)

LIGHT LEVEL: SHADE · PART SHADE · SUN

SOIL MOISTURE LEVEL: WET · MEDIUM · DRY

LIFESTYLE: EARLY ESTABLISHER · KEEN COMPETITOR · RESOURCEFUL SCAVENGER

HEIGHT: 6-12 IN

SPREAD: 4-12 IN

Goldenseal

Hydrastis canadensis

This ground cover plant gets its name from its characteristic yellow roots and sap. Its large, wrinkly, and distinctively palmate pubescent leaves give way to a white flower that emerges from the leaf base in late spring to early summer. Bright red berry-like fruits follow soon after and provide food for woodland birds.

Goldenseal can be grown by seed, but spreads most commonly by rhizomes. Though highly sought after for various medicinal purposes—including as an antibiotic and anti-inflammatory—this species is also an important woodland pollinator plant.

Occasionally available in nurseries and not difficult to grow from seed, goldenseal does require some patience. Seeds must be kept moist and require a winter cold period, and prefer more alkaline soils.

Naturally ranging throughout eastern North America, goldenseal is considered rare, threatened or endangered in most of the Northeast. Populations are increasingly threatened by over-foraging, so be careful not to purchase wild collected plants.

ALSO TRY: Wild ginger (*Asarum canadense*)

LIGHT LEVEL: SHADE | PART SHADE | SUN

SOIL MOISTURE LEVEL: WET | MEDIUM | DRY

LIFESTYLE: EARLY ESTABLISHER | KEEN COMPETITOR | RESOURCEFUL SCAVENGER

HEIGHT: 6–20 IN

SPREAD: 8–14 IN

Red columbine

Aquilegia canadensis

Red columbine's striking crimson flowers with yellow centers provide hearty food for pollinators, and is a favorite of hummingbirds, long-tongued bees, moths, and butterflies. Pale bluish leaves provide food for the columbine duskywing butterfly and the columbine leafminer.

This species grows with a fascinating duality. It handles some of the most challenging conditions, from full sun to full shade, ledge rock gardens to deep pine needles. But put it where it doesn't want to be, and it won't stay long. When in the right location, this short-lived perennial will reseed readily and has a habit of moving around a garden space until it has found its preferred spot. Does not compete well in a crowded garden.

Many *Aquilegia* spp. and cultivars are available in the nursery trade, but be careful to choose the species that will support the wildlife in your region. Easy to propagate by seed. Sow outside in the fall or winter; requires at least sixty days of cold period for germination.

ALSO TRY: Wild geranium (*Geranium maculatum*)

LIGHT LEVEL: SHADE · PART SHADE · SUN

SOIL MOISTURE LEVEL: WET · MEDIUM · DRY

LIFESTYLE: EARLY ESTABLISHER · KEEN COMPETITOR · RESOURCEFUL SCAVENGER

HEIGHT: 2–3 FT

SPREAD: 10–18 IN

Downy skullcap

Scutellaria incana

Downy skullcap is named after its soft, hairy leaves and saucer-shaped calyx. Long-lasting deep to powder blue tubular blooms attract bumble bees and other pollinators from mid-summer into fall. Leaves often turn an attractive burgundy towards the end of season.

This versatile and adaptable plant spreads readily by seed and rhizome, and can make an attractive specimen in a wide range of garden spaces, including pollinator gardens, rain gardens, and potted planters. Does best in well-drained sandy soil, but tolerates clay and is resilient to drought and compaction as well. Generally distasteful to deer and rabbits.

Though not readily available in garden centers, this species is easy to collect and propagate by seed, which is available from several reputable sources. Store dry and plant in fall or winter for spring germination. Naturally found in upland rocky forests and woodland edges throughout much of eastern North America.

ALSO TRY: Showy skullcap (*Scutellaria serrata*); Northeast beardtongue (*Penstemon hirsutus*)

LIGHT LEVEL: SHADE | **PART SHADE** | SUN

SOIL MOISTURE LEVEL: WET | **MEDIUM** | **DRY**

LIFESTYLE: EARLY ESTABLISHER | KEEN COMPETITOR | **RESOURCEFUL SCAVENGER**

HEIGHT: 1-3 FT

SPREAD: 12-18 IN

Woodland sunflower

Helianthus divaricatus

Sunflowers (*Helianthus* spp.) largely hail from North America and are well known for their large composite flowers that, in some cases, track the daily arc of the sun.

Naturally found in dry, open woods and forest edges, woodland sunflower is one of the best suited sunflowers for dry shade. This perennial produces up to three-inch-wide yellow flowers that bloom between July and September at the top of a branched stem. Sunflowers are second only to goldenrods in terms of the number of pollen specialist bee species they attract. Woodland sunflower feeds the striking sunflower burrowing-resin bee (pictured), sunflower mining bee, yellow-faced miner bee, and denticulate longhorn bee. Woodland sunflower is also one of the preferred nectar sources for the federally endangered Karner blue butterfly.

Perennial sunflowers spread vigorously by shallow rhizomes; plant with caution in small landscapes. Curb spread by dividing every three to four years or plant alongside barriers like paving stones. This wildflower would also be an eye-catching addition to a large container.

ALSO TRY: Ten-petal sunflower (*Helianthus decapetalus*)

LIGHT LEVEL: SHADE, **PART SHADE**, SUN

SOIL MOISTURE LEVEL: WET, **MEDIUM**, **DRY**

LIFESTYLE: **EARLY ESTABLISHER**, **KEEN COMPETITOR**, RESOURCEFUL SCAVENGER

HEIGHT 2-5 FT

SPREAD 1-3 FT

Poke milkweed

Asclepias exaltata

This lesser-known milkweed species is the only one native to Maine that grows well in deep shade. Its elongated, droopy leaves feed many insects, including caterpillars of the milkweed tussock moth (pictured) and rapidly vanishing monarch butterfly. Small greenish-white to dusty pink flowers affixed to long dangling pedicels bloom in late spring to early summer, before other native milkweeds. These early blooms feed myriad woodland pollinators when not much else is available.

Long, narrow seed pods split open to reveal many silk laden seeds. Not an aggressive spreader like some milkweeds, and easily propagated by seed. Store seeds dry and sow outdoors in fall and winter.

This tall milkweed species prefers average to acidic soils. Be sure to provide adequate leaf litter as this plant thrives in soils with high organic matter.

LIGHT LEVEL: SHADE, PART SHADE, SUN

SOIL MOISTURE LEVEL: WET, MEDIUM, DRY

LIFESTYLE: EARLY ESTABLISHER, KEEN COMPETITOR, RESOURCEFUL SCAVENGER

HEIGHT: 2-5 FT

SPREAD: 1-2 FT

Broad-leaved sedge

Carex platyphylla

With exceptionally wide, semi-evergreen foliage covered in a distinctive blueish-silver cast, broad-leaved sedge is one of the easiest sedges to identify. This small, clump-forming woodland sedge grows happily in dry shade and can be found scattered in rich deciduous forests, wooded slopes, and rocky ravines.

By May, several slender flowering stalks emerge from the basal foliage, each topped with dark staminate spikes bearing large, cream-colored anthers. The wind-pollinated pistillate spikes form clusters of seeds by late spring, each wrapped in an egg-shaped covering. The seeds provide food for sparrows, wild turkeys, and ruffed grouse. Rabbits and deer tend to ignore woodland sedges.

The attractive foliage and early blooms of broad-leaved sedge pair beautifully with spring ephemerals, adding interest to just about any woodland garden. Growing sedges from seed can be difficult. Sow on the soil surface, keep moist, and be patient. Germination can take many months.

ALSO TRY: Plantain-leaved sedge (*Carex plantaginea*); white-tinged sedge (*C. albicans*)

LIGHT LEVEL: SHADE · PART SHADE · SUN

SOIL MOISTURE LEVEL: WET · MEDIUM · DRY

LIFESTYLE: EARLY ESTABLISHER · KEEN COMPETITOR · RESOURCEFUL SCAVENGER

HEIGHT: 6–12 IN

SPREAD: 8–12 IN

Eastern wahoo

Euonymus atropurpureus

This large deciduous shrub has an upright form with a spreading, irregular crown. Usually single-stemmed, eastern wahoo spreads by long rhizomes to form loose thickets along forest edges, wooded slopes, and stream banks. But unlike its notorious relatives—winged burning bush (*E. alatus*) and Asian bittersweet (*Celastrus orbiculatus*)—eastern wahoo does not aggressively spread at the expense of native species. This makes it a good replacement for winged burning bush.

Eastern wahoo is a remarkable plant throughout the year. In late spring, clusters of small, maroon flowers hang from delicate branches. These distinctive, four-petaled blooms produce a fermenting fruit-like scent to attract their preferred pollinator, fungus gnats. Striking pink-red fruit capsules follow in the fall, each opening to reveal bright red arils (covered seeds) that serve as edible enticements for animals. Foliage turns greenish red and yellow before falling to expose the shrub's unusual green bark with gray striping in the winter.

ALSO TRY: Bladdernut (*Staphylea trifolia*)

LIGHT LEVEL: SHADE | **PART SHADE** | SUN

SOIL MOISTURE LEVEL: WET | **MEDIUM** | DRY

LIFESTYLE: EARLY ESTABLISHER | KEEN COMPETITOR | **RESOURCEFUL SCAVENGER**

HEIGHT: 12–20 FT

SPREAD: 8–10 FT

Scarlet oak

Quercus coccinea

True to its name, the deeply lobed leaves of this majestic oak turn a stunning scarlet (occasionally yellow-brown) in the fall. Among the fastest growing oaks when young, scarlet oak is also among the shortest-lived (80 years).

Oaks are well known for their sporadic yet coordinated production of acorns, a phenomenon known as mast seeding. By alternating through periods of seed scarcity and abundance, oaks starve and subsequently satiate seed predators like acorn weevils, increasing the number of viable acorns that get dispersed.

An enormous variety of animals depend on oaks for food and shelter. Walking sticks, leaf beetles, gall wasp larvae, and hundreds of species of Lepidoptera eat the leaves, including Edward's hairstreak (pictured), Juvenal's duskywing skipper, and imperial moth. Many songbirds nest in the broad crown of scarlet oak, including scarlet tanager, eastern wood-pewee, and yellow-throated vireo.

Although seedlings tolerate part-shade, scarlet oak becomes increasingly shade intolerant as it matures. More shade tolerant options include black and northern red oak.

ALSO TRY: Black oak (*Quercus velutina*); northern red oak (*Q. rubra*)

LIGHT LEVEL: SHADE · PART SHADE · SUN

SOIL MOISTURE LEVEL: WET · MEDIUM · DRY

LIFESTYLE: EARLY ESTABLISHER · KEEN COMPETITOR · RESOURCEFUL SCAVENGER

HEIGHT: 50–70 FT

SPREAD: 25–40 FT

Native Plant Species

Shady, medium-to-wet

Carolina spring beauty

Claytonia caroliniana

Diminutive yet delightful, Carolina spring beauty is one of our earliest flowering spring ephemerals. The leaves emerge from under their winter blanket of leaf mulch to make the most of the spring sun before the trees overhead leaf out.

The small, delicate flowers have five white petals with faint to prominent pink veins that serve as nectar guides. Flowers are diurnal, closing at night and on cloudy days to shield their valuable pink pollen. Spring beauty miner bees avidly collect this pollen and are the primary pollinator. Greater bee flies, blow flies, and flower flies (pictured) also visit to sip nectar. Once pollinated, spring beauty promptly sets seed and sets off for dormancy, with the visible parts of the plant withering away until next spring.

This charming perennial will slowly spread vegetatively and by seed. Stems arise from a small, starchy tuber that is beloved by small rodents. Protect establishing plants with quarter-inch hardware cloth buried a half-foot underground.

ALSO TRY: Virginia spring beauty (*Claytonia virginica*)

LIGHT LEVEL: SHADE, PART SHADE, SUN

SOIL MOISTURE LEVEL: WET, MEDIUM, DRY

LIFESTYLE: EARLY ESTABLISHER, KEEN COMPETITOR, RESOURCEFUL SCAVENGER

HEIGHT: 2-6 IN

SPREAD: 4-6 IN

Large-flowered bellwort

Uvularia grandiflora

Also known as merrybells, large-flowered bellwort is named for its drooping pale to golden yellow bell-shaped flowers that emerge on individual stems in early spring. A larger relative of the more commonly found sessile-leaved bellwort (*U. sessilifolia*), this small perennial provides a bounty of pollen and nectar for early spring pollinators such as mason, sweat, and mining bees (including the rare bellwort mining bee).

Attractive long and silky leaves provide beautiful forest ground cover. Large-flowered bellwort will slowly spread by rhizomes and can grow to form colonies, creating a beautiful massing effect in shade gardens. This species is a great replacement for ornamental spring bulbs and pips like fritillaries and lily of the valley (*Convallaria majalis*).

Growing from seed is possible but takes a bit of work; seeds cannot be stored dry but, instead, must be sown fresh outdoors and will take two winters to break dormancy. Seed and root stock are available from reputable sellers.

ALSO TRY: Sessile-leaved bellwort (*Uvularia sessilifolia*); wild ginger (*Asarum canadense*)

LIGHT LEVEL: SHADE · PART SHADE · SUN

SOIL MOISTURE LEVEL: WET · MEDIUM · DRY

LIFESTYLE: EARLY ESTABLISHER · KEEN COMPETITOR · RESOURCEFUL SCAVENGER

HEIGHT: 12-18 IN

SPREAD: 12-18 IN

Red baneberry

Actaea rubra

A beautiful perennial for the woodland understory, this spring blooming species produces joyful white plumy flower clusters that provide pollen to sweat bees, flies, and beetles. The brilliant red fruits that follow are enjoyed by birds, but toxic to humans and other mammals. With attractive, pinnately compound leaves, red baneberry makes a great specimen for shade gardens and a useful replacement for common garden plants like astilbe.

Red baneberry isn't very common in the nursery trade but is available through reputable native plant growers. It can also be grown from seed if patient, as it requires two cold periods to germinate. A less common white-fruited form (*A. rubra* var. *neglecta*) has more of a shrubby shape and growth habit with ornate leaves.

ALSO TRY: Doll's eyes (*Actaea pachypoda*)

LIGHT LEVEL: SHADE, PART SHADE, SUN

SOIL MOISTURE LEVEL: WET, MEDIUM, DRY

LIFESTYLE: EARLY ESTABLISHER, KEEN COMPETITOR, RESOURCEFUL SCAVENGER

HEIGHT: 1–3 FT

SPREAD: 12–18 IN

Virginia bluebells

Mertensia virginica

Possessing an almost ethereal beauty, this spring ephemeral grows adorned with tender blue-green leaves and loose clusters of soothing, pink-purple buds and sky-blue flowers. These trumpet-shaped blossoms support queen bumble bees and other early spring pollinators, including digger bees, mason bees, butterflies, skippers, and sphinx moths. Hummingbirds may also occasionally visit the flowers, which bloom for about three weeks between April and May. Foliage dies to the ground by mid-summer.

Virginia bluebells readily self-seeds once established, forming large groupings that serve as a beautiful woodland ground cover. As with most spring ephemerals, bluebells prefer sites that start off sunny in the spring and turn shady by summer. Pairs well with ferns, foamflower (*Tiarella cordifolia*), phlox (*Phlox divaricata*), and other woodland perennials that remain active through summer.

Although Virginia bluebells is not native to most of the Northeast, its equally attractive sibling seaside bluebells (*M. maritima*) commonly grows along Maine's coast.

ALSO TRY: Eastern waterleaf (*Hydrophyllum virginianum*)

LIGHT LEVEL: SHADE, PART SHADE, SUN

SOIL MOISTURE LEVEL: WET, MEDIUM, DRY

LIFESTYLE: EARLY ESTABLISHER, KEEN COMPETITOR, RESOURCEFUL SCAVENGER

HEIGHT: 18–24 IN

SPREAD: 12–18 IN

Blue lobelia

Lobelia siphilitica

A pollinator magnet, blue lobelia supports everything from bees to hummingbirds. Long-lasting light- to deep-blue flowers emerge stacked up tall stalks with blooms that persist through late summer.

This short-lived perennial produces massive amounts of seed and will readily spread into open areas in a garden. Seeds ripen over time and are easily collected when seed heads are brown, dry, and split open.

This adaptable plant can handle occasional flooding and dry conditions, making it especially useful in an unpredictable climate and well-suited for containers. Seeds require light and sixty days of cold to germinate. Easy to grow from seed and often available in garden centers. Due to their attraction to pollinators, it is important to purchase blue lobelia from growers who do not use pesticides.

ALSO TRY: Cardinal flower (*Lobelia cardinalis*)

LIGHT LEVEL: SHADE · PART SHADE · SUN

SOIL MOISTURE LEVEL: WET · MEDIUM · DRY

LIFESTYLE: EARLY ESTABLISHER · KEEN COMPETITOR · RESOURCEFUL SCAVENGER

HEIGHT: 2–3 FT

SPREAD: 12–16 IN

White snakeroot

Ageratina altissima

Often found in rich deciduous forests along waterways, this short-lived perennial bears bright-white clusters of fuzzy flowers that attract pollinators from July through October. A prolific self-seeder, white snakeroot is an excellent species to replace non-native aggressive woodland species. Curtail spread by trimming off spent blooms.

Toxic to humans, livestock, and other mammals if ingested. Although studies have shown livestock need to regularly eat large amounts to reach toxic levels, avoid planting white snakeroot in areas frequented by pets. Deer largely avoid it for this reason.

ALSO TRY: Blue wood-aster (*Symphyotrichum cordifolium*)

LIGHT LEVEL: SHADE, PART SHADE, SUN

SOIL MOISTURE LEVEL: WET, MEDIUM, DRY

LIFESTYLE: EARLY ESTABLISHER, KEEN COMPETITOR, RESOURCEFUL SCAVENGER

HEIGHT: 2–3 FT

SPREAD: 2–3 FT

Bog goldenrod

Solidago uliginosa

Bog goldenrod has smooth leaves that clasp a sturdy, often deep red stem. Flower shape varies, but late summer yellow blooms usually have dense, slender plumes that rise high above the foliage.

A magnet for caterpillars and pollinators, goldenrods also attract insectivorous songbirds, predatory wasps, and ambush bugs. One of the few goldenrods that thrives in wet soil, bog goldenrod makes a lovely addition to most any spot with acidic soil, from sun-drenched rain gardens to moist and shady borders. Dappled shade will curb spread by rhizomes.

ALSO TRY: Zigzag goldenrod (*Solidago flexicaulis*)

LIGHT LEVEL: SHADE, PART SHADE, SUN

SOIL MOISTURE LEVEL: WET, MEDIUM, DRY

LIFESTYLE: EARLY ESTABLISHER, KEEN COMPETITOR, RESOURCEFUL SCAVENGER

HEIGHT: 2–5 FT

SPREAD: 2–4 FT

Orange jewelweed

Impatiens capensis

Commonly forming large, dense stands in low woodlands and along streams and roadside ditches, this charming annual gets its common name from the sparkling droplets that often collect on its bluish-green, water repellent leaves.

Orange jewelweed blooms from July through October, producing bright orange, two-lipped flowers that hang from slender stalks. The red-orange spotting, if present, is often concentrated on the flower's lower lip, creating an enticing landing pad for butterflies and long-tongued bees. Hummingbirds are the primary pollinator, though, and rely on the spurred flowers as a major source of late summer nectar. Occasionally, cunning bumble bees will chew holes near the spur to access nectar.

Flowers are followed by pale green seedpods that, once ripe, burst open with the slightest touch, giving rise to the plant's other name: touch-me-not. Orange jewelweed tolerates periodic flooding and some dry shade. Although not preferred by deer, expect browsed plants where deer pressure is high.

ALSO TRY: Pale jewelweed (*Impatiens pallida*)

LIGHT LEVEL: SHADE, PART SHADE, SUN

SOIL MOISTURE LEVEL: WET, MEDIUM, DRY

LIFESTYLE: EARLY ESTABLISHER, KEEN COMPETITOR, RESOURCEFUL SCAVENGER

HEIGHT: 2-5 FT

SPREAD: 1-2 FT

This vase-shaped fern forms dense clumps of fine-textured fronds with green to reddish-brown rachis (stems). Distinctive dark brown scales adorn the emerging fiddleheads and, later on, the stalks of each frond.

Northern lady fern is quite adaptable, tolerating sun if sheltered from the wind and in soil that stays consistently moist. The shallow roots are intolerant of trampling and drought, though. Clumps provide significant wildlife cover, and larvae of the bronze feather-legged moth feed on the spores.

ALSO TRY: Silvery false spleenwort (*Deparia acrostichoides*)

Northern lady fern

Athyrium angustum

LIGHT LEVEL: SHADE, PART SHADE, SUN

SOIL MOISTURE LEVEL: WET, MEDIUM, DRY

LIFESTYLE: EARLY ESTABLISHER, KEEN COMPETITOR, RESOURCEFUL SCAVENGER

HEIGHT: 1–3 FT

SPREAD: 12–18 IN

A ground cover that loves deep shade, broad beech fern forms loose groupings by creeping rhizomes. Its unique foliage has downward-pointing leaflets at the base of each broad, triangular frond that turns yellow in fall.

This late-rising, deciduous fern often doesn't emerge until well into May, making it an excellent companion to spring ephemerals. Although tolerant of quite dry soils, broad beech fern grows best in moist, acidic soil that is rich in organic matter. Like many ferns, it benefits from leaf mulch.

ALSO TRY: Long beech fern (*Phegopteris connectilis*)

Broad beech fern

Phegopteris hexagonoptera

LIGHT LEVEL: SHADE, PART SHADE, SUN

SOIL MOISTURE LEVEL: WET, MEDIUM, DRY

LIFESTYLE: EARLY ESTABLISHER, KEEN COMPETITOR, RESOURCEFUL SCAVENGER

HEIGHT: 12–18 IN

SPREAD: 1–3 FT

Sweet azalea

Rhododendron arborescens

Also known as smooth azalea, this beautiful deciduous shrub has whitish pink spring blooms with deep red stamens and pistils that produce an incredible sweet cinnamon fragrance in late spring to early summer. Many pollinators enjoy these flowers, including the rare specialist azalea mining bee. Come fall, shining green foliage turns attractive yellow to red.

Though this plant is toxic to humans, deer will browse on it and several caterpillar species feed on it as well, including the laurel sphinx and promethea moth. Thrives in moist, well-drained soils. Slow to grow from seed but will spread fast by runners once established. Laying down a thick layer of leaf litter will help this plant thrive in a shade garden or shrub border.

Not commonly found in garden centers, sweet azalea grows wonderfully in garden settings and is naturally found in woodlands and stream banks with sandy acidic soils.

ALSO TRY: Swamp azalea (*Rhododendron viscosum*); early azalea (*R. prinophyllum*)

LIGHT LEVEL: SHADE · **PART SHADE** · SUN

SOIL MOISTURE LEVEL: WET · **MEDIUM** · DRY

LIFESTYLE: EARLY ESTABLISHER · KEEN COMPETITOR · **RESOURCEFUL SCAVENGER**

HEIGHT 8–15 FT

SPREAD 8–15 FT

Yellow buckeye

Aesculus flava

Admired for its large, upright clusters of creamy yellow flowers that bloom in late spring, yellow buckeye is native to protected, cove forests and river bottoms of the central Appalachians. Pollinated by hummingbirds and various long-tongued bees, its flowers are followed by its familiar fruit: shiny, chestnut-brown nuts marked with a single tan spot (the 'buckeye') and enclosed in a smooth, leathery husk. The nuts are inedible but make pleasing good luck charms.

As the largest North American buckeye species, yellow buckeye is a great shade tree. It's one of the first trees to leaf out in the spring and senesce in autumn; the palmate leaves turn an attractive yellow-green to burnt orange in September.

Yellow buckeye prefers moist, fertile soils that are rich in organic matter. Protect from the wind to minimize leaf scorch. This tree makes an excellent alternative to the non-native horse-chestnut (*A. hippocastanum*), a popular ornamental that is more susceptible to leaf blight.

ALSO TRY: Ohio buckeye (*Aesculus glabra*)

LIGHT LEVEL: SHADE | **PART SHADE** | **SUN**

SOIL MOISTURE LEVEL: WET | **MEDIUM** | DRY

LIFESTYLE: EARLY ESTABLISHER | **KEEN COMPETITOR** | RESOURCEFUL SCAVENGER

HEIGHT: 50–80 FT

SPREAD: 25–40 FT

Bibliography

Books & Publications

Baisden, Emily C., Douglas W. Tallamy, Desiree L. Narango, and Eileen Boyle. 2018. "Do Cultivars of Native Plants Support Insect Herbivores?" *HortTechnology* 28 (5): 596–606. https://doi.org/10.21273/HORTTECH03957-18.

Eckberg, James, Eric Lee-Mäder, Jennifer Hopwood, Sarah Foltz Jordan, and Brianna Borders. 2017. *Native Thistles: A Conservation Practitioner's Guide. Plant Ecology, Seed Production Methods, and Habitat Restoration Opportunities.* Portland, OR: Xerces Society for Invertebrate Conservation. https://xerces.org/sites/default/files/2018-05/16-029_01_XercesSoc_Native-Thistles-Conservation-Guide_web.pdf.

Erickson, E., R.R. Junker, J.G. Ali, N. McCartney, H.M. Patch, and C.M. Grozinger. 2022. "Complex Floral Traits Shape Pollinator Attraction to Ornamental Plants." Annals of Botany 130 (4): 561–77. https://doi.org/10.1093/aob/mcac082.

Faegri, Knut, and L. van der Pijl. 2016. *The Principles of Pollination Ecology*. 3rd rev. ed. Oxford; New York: Pergamon Press.

Friedman, Jannice. 2020. "The Evolution of Annual and Perennial Plant Life Histories: Ecological Correlates and Genetic Mechanisms." *Annual Review of Ecology, Evolution, and Systematics* 51 (1): 461–81. https://doi.org/10.1146/annurev-ecolsys-110218-024638.

Gawler, Susan C., and Andrew Cutko. 2010. *Natural Landscapes of Maine: A Guide to Natural Communities and Ecosystems*. Revised and updated edition 2018. Augusta, ME: Maine Natural Areas Program, Maine Department of Agriculture, Conservation, and Forestry.

Hanley, Mick E., Byron B. Lamont, Meredith M. Fairbanks, and Christine M. Rafferty. 2007. "Plant Structural Traits and Their Role in Anti-Herbivore Defence." *Perspectives in Plant Ecology, Evolution and Systematics* 8 (4): 157–78. https://doi.org/10.1016/j.ppees.2007.01.001.

Hulting, Katherine A., Lindsey R. Kemmerling, Sean R. Griffin, Jessica Webb, Ally K. Brown, and Nick M. Haddad. 2024. "Seed Mix Design and Floral Resources Drive Multitrophic Interactions in Prairie Restoration." *Journal of Applied Ecology* 61 (4): 859–68. https://doi.org/10.1111/1365-2664.14605.

Pierce, Simon, Daniel Negreiros, Bruno E. L. Cerabolini, et al. 2017. "A Global Method for Calculating Plant CSR Ecological Strategies Applied Across Biomes World-wide." *Functional Ecology* 31 (2): 444–57. https://doi.org/10.1111/1365-2435.12722.

Ricker, Jacob G., Jessica D. Lubell, and Mark H. Brand. 2019. "Comparing Insect Pollinator Visitation for Six Native Shrub Species and Their Cultivars." *HortScience* 54 (11): 2086–90. https://doi.org/10.21273/HORTSCI14375-19.

Rose, Jeffrey P., and Kenneth J. Sytsma. 2021. "Complex Interactions Underlie the Correlated Evolution of Floral Traits and Their Association with Pollinators in a Clade with Diverse Pollination Systems." *Evolution* 75 (6): 1431–49. https://doi.org/10.1111/evo.14220.

Thompson, Elizabeth H., Eric R. Sorenson, and Robert J. Zaino. 2019. *Wetland, Woodland, Wildland: A Guide to the Natural Communities of Vermont*. 2nd ed. White River Junction, VT: Chelsea Green Publishing.

Wan, Nian-Feng, Liwan Fu, Matteo Dainese, et al. 2022. "Plant Genetic Diversity Affects Multiple Trophic Levels and Trophic Interactions." *Nature Communications* 13 (1): 7312. https://doi.org/10.1038/s41467-022-35087-7.

Xie, Yingying, Hanna T. Thammavong, and Daniel S. Park. 2022. "The Ecological Implications of Intra- and Inter-species Variation in Phenological Sensitivity." *New Phytologist* 236 (2): 760–73. https://doi.org/10.1111/nph.18361.

Websites

Adirondacks Forever Wild: wildadirondacks.org

Butterflies and Moths of North America: butterfliesandmoths.org

Garden Plant Finder, Native Plant Trust: plantfinder.nativeplanttrust.org/plant-search

Go Botany, Native Plant Trust: gobotany.nativeplanttrust.org

Illinois Wildflowers: illinoiswildflowers.info

Maine Natural Areas Program, Maine Department of Agriculture, Conservation and Forestry: maine.gov/dacf/mnap

Mass Moths: massmoths.org

Minnesota Wildflowers: minnesotawildflowers.info

Native Plant Finder for Pollinator Species at Risk, Gegear Lab at UMass Dartmouth: gegearlab.weebly.com/plant-list.html

Plant Finder, Missouri Botanical Garden: missouribotanicalgarden.org/plantfinder/plantfindersearch.aspx

Pollinator-Friendly Native Plant Lists, Xerces Society: xerces.org/pollinator-conservation/pollinator-friendly-plant-lists

Resource Library, Wild Seed Project: wildseedproject.net/blog

The Bees of Vermont, Vermont Center for Ecostudies: val.vtecostudies.org/projects/vtbees/bees-of-vt

Wabanaki REACH: wabanakireach.org

Recommended Reading

Queer Literature

Angus, Callum. 2021. *A Natural History of Transition.* Montreal, Quebec: Metonymy Press.

Imbler, Sabrina. 2022. *How Far the Light Reaches: A Life in Ten Sea Creatures.* New York: Little, Brown and Company.

Mortimer-Sandilands, Catriona, and Bruce Erickson, eds. 2011. *Queer Ecologies: Sex, Nature, Politics, Desire.* Bloomington, IN.: Indiana University Press.

Parreñas, Juno Salazar, and Nicole Seymour. 2022. "Afterword: Ecological Inqueeries." *Environmental Humanities* 14 (3): 718–25. https://doi.org/10.1215/22011919-9962992.

Seymour, Nicole, ed. 2013. Strange Natures: *Futurity, Empathy, and the Queer Ecological Imagination.* Urbana, IL: University of Illinois Press.

Indigenous Knowledge

Kimmerer, Robin Wall. 2024. *The Serviceberry: Abundance and Reciprocity in the Natural World.* 1st ed. New York: Scribner.

Ostendorf-Rodríguez, Yasmine. 2023. *Let's Become Fungal! Mycelium Teachings and the Arts: Based on Conversations with Indigenous Wisdom Keepers, Artists, Curators, Feminists, and Mycologists.* Amsterdam: Valiz.

Subramaniam, Banu. 2024. *Botany of Empire: Plant Worlds and the Scientific Legacies of Colonialism.* Feminist Technosciences. Seattle, WA: University of Washington Press.

Yunkaporta, Tyson. 2020. *Sand Talk: How Indigenous Thinking Can Save the World.* San Francisco, CA: HarperOne.

Gardening

Holm, Heather. 2017. *Bees: An Identification and Native Plant Forage Guide.* Minnetonka, MN: Pollination Press.

Holm, Heather. 2014. *Pollinators of Native Plants: Attract, Observe and Identify Pollinators and Beneficial Insects with Native Plants.* Minnetonka, MN: Pollination Press.

Holm, Heather. 2021. *Wasps: Their Biology, Diversity, and Role as Beneficial Insects and Pollinators of Native Plants.* Minnetonka, MN: Pollination Press.

Lorimer, Uli, and Native Plant Trust. 2022. *The Northeast Native Plant Primer.* Portland, OR: Timber Press.

Rainer, Thomas, and Claudia West. 2015. *Planting in a Post-Wild World: Designing Plant Communities for Resilient Landscapes.* Portland, OR: Timber Press.

Tallamy, Douglas W. 2009. *Bringing Nature Home: How You Can Sustain Wildlife with Native Plants.* Updated and Expanded pbk. ed. Portland, OR: Timber Press.

Tallamy, Douglas W. 2019. *Nature's Best Hope: A New Approach to Conservation That Starts in Your Yard.* Portland, OR: Timber Press.

The Xerces Society. 2011. *Attractive Native Pollinators: Protecting North America's Bees and Butterflies.* North Adams, MA: Storey Publishing.

The Xerces Society. 2016. *Gardening for Butterflies: How You Can Attract and Protect Beautiful, Beneficial Insects.* Portland, OR: Timber Press.

Vogt, Benjamin. 2023. *Prairie Up: An Introduction to Natural Garden Design.* Urbana, IL.: 3 Fields Books.

Image Credits

Photos not noted here are © Emily Baisden, © Heather McCargo, or © Tyler Refsland, courtesy of Wild Seed Project.

Cover and inside art

Julian Plum, gouache and colored pencil (julianplum.com)

INSIDE COVER Leatherwood: © Alan Cressler

2 Bloodroot and yellow trout lily: © Lisa Looke

4 Narrow-leaved mountain mint: © Dan Jaffe Wilder

6 Blunt-lobed hepatica: © Alan Cressler

8 Annual pollinator cover crop at The Farm Between, Jeffersonville, VT: © John Hayden

10 Pratt, Anne and Step, Edward. Nightshade, thorn apple, and henbane. 1905: Public Domain

12 Toan, Frankie. Holding Living Things. 2020, Claude Haus Summer Solstice, Denver: © Wes Magyar

14 Wild clematis: © Lisa Looke

20 From top to bottom: Bee-like flower scarab beetle on white meadowsweet: © Logan Ullrich; Bumble bee and American copper butterfly on green-headed coneflower: © Mary Anne Borge; Eastern carpenter bee on spotted bee balm: © Heather Holm; Showy tick-trefoil: © Joshua Mayer**

21 From top to bottom: Mining bee on Dutchman's breeches: © Heather Holm; Flower fly on yellow prairie grass: © Chris Helzer; Black and gold bumble bee on blueberry: © Heather Holm; Thread-waisted wasp on butterfly milkweed: © Heather Holm; Ruby-throated hummingbird on trumpet honeysuckle: © Thomas Shahan*

22 From top to bottom: Bearberry leaves: © Katy Chayka; Grasshopper on sedge: © Joshua Mayer**; Field thistle flower head: © Katy Chayka

23 From top to bottom: Cinnamon fern fiddleheads: © Dan Jaffe Wilder; Spicebush swallowtail caterpillar: by Ryan Hagerty, Public Domain; Sawfly larvae: © Margaret Anne Miles

24 Native seeds: © Lisa Looke

25 Eastern waterleaf (var. *atranthum*; top left): © Alan Cressler; Eastern waterleaf (var. *virginianum*; bottom left): © Michelle Norcéide*; Switchgrass ecotypes (right): © Grace John

26 Spring beauty miner bee (left): © Judy Gallagher*; Virginia spring beauty white morph (right): © Doug McGrady*

27 Ninebark calligrapha beetle (top): © Jorie O'Brien; Ninebark 'Diabolo' (bottom): © David Stang**

28 Wildflower meadow at Rider Park, PA: © Nicholas Tonelli*

36 Narrow-leaved mountain mint and black-eyed coneflower: © Dan Jaffe Wilder

38 Field pussytoes pistillate flowers (top): © Lisa Looke; Staminate flowers: © Doug McGrady*

40 Wood betony flowers: © Dan Jaffe Wilder; Leaves: © mayfly1963* (inaturalist.org)

41 Canada milk vetch flowers: © Gwen Senio

42 Field of sundial lupine: © Adam Balzer; Karner blue: © Terry Mortier; Leaves: © Joshua Mayer**

43 Narrow-leaved sundrop blooms: © Dan Jaffe Wilder; Primrose moth caterpillar: © Reiner Jakubowski**

44 Narrow-leaved mountain mint with great golden digger wasp: © Dan Jaffe Wilder; Wild bee-balm: © Dan Jaffe Wilder

45 Pink corydalis seed pods: © Martha B. Moss courtesy of Native Gardens of Blue Hill (nativemainegardens.org)

46 Foxglove beardtongue fruit capsules and flower close-up: © Uli Lorimer

47 Hoary vervain flowers: © Aaron Carlson**; Fruiting spikes: © Kevin and Sue Hanley, chdphoto (inaturalist.org)

48 Sideoats grama flowers: © Kevin and Sue Hanley, chdphoto (inaturalist.org); Form: © Colorado Springs Utilities

49 Kalm's brome spikelets: © Mark Kluge§

51 Gray birch stems: © Shaun Pogacnik§; Staminate catkin: © Randi V. Wilfert Eckel, Toadshade Wildflower Farm (toadshade.com)

52 Meadow garden in Garden in the Woods, Framingham, MA: © Uli Lorimer

54 Beetberry fruit (top): © Arthur Goldsmith (artnatureculture .blogspot.com); Leaves: © Ed Poropat§; Common sootywing skipper larvae on lambsquarters © Sara Bright

55 Showy tick-trefoil flowers (top): © John Hagstrom; Flower close-up: © Chris Helzer; Fruit: © Peter M. Dziuk

56 Swamp thistle form (top): © David Schwaegler; Bumble bees on flower: © Joshua Mayer**

57 Licorice goldenrod blooms: © Dan Jaffe Wilder

58 Green-headed coneflower: © Dan Jaffe Wilder; Hollow Joe-Pye weed: © Lisa Looke

59 Canada wild rye seed heads (top): © Wayne Washam; Frosty seed head: © Peter C. Gorman

60 Shortbeak sedge: © Prairie Moon Nursery (prairiemoon.com); Fringed sedge: © Adriel Diver

61 Trumpet honeysuckle flowers (top): © Dave Govoni; Fruit: © Dan Jaffe Wilder

62 Large cranberry form (top): © Doug McGrady*; Flowers: © Dan Jaffe Wilder; Fruit: © Glen Mittelhauser

63 Swamp rose with slender longhorn and tumbling flower beetles (top): © Uli Lorimer

64 Silky dogwood flowers (top): © Adriel Diver; Leaves: © Sara Rall§; Fruit: © Lisa Looke

65 Pinxterbloom azalea: © Michael Newlon*; Maleberry flowers and fruit: © Siddarth Machado

66 Silky willow form (top): © Salicicola.com (Alexey Zinovjev and Irina Kadis); Red-tailed mining bee on Salix spp: © Spencer Hardy; Acadian hairstreak on Salix spp: © Keith A. Wickens

67 Tamarack form (top): © Dan Jaffe Wilder; Seed cones: © Uli Lorimer

68 Blue-stemmed goldenrod: © Tom Potterfield

70 Partridgeberry (all): © Lisa Looke

71 Bloodroot flowers (top): © Lisa Looke; Unfurling leaf: © Dan Jaffe Wilder

72 Goldenseal form with fruit (top): © Uli Lorimer; Flowers: © Dan Jaffe Wilder

73 Red columbine form (top): © Uli Lorimer; Flower: © Alan Cressler

74 Downy skullcap (top): © Brian Ellis; Flower with small carpenter bee: © Mary Anne Borge

75 Sunflower burrowing-resin bee on woodland sunflower (top): © Spencer Hardy; Flowers: © Emily Oglesby / North Carolina Botanical Garden

76 Poke milkweed and milkweed tussock moth (all): Alan Cressler

---

*CC-BY 4.0

**CC-BY-SA 4.0

§CC-BY-NC 4.0

https://creativecommons.org/licenses

77 Broad-leaved sedge form: © Michael Nerrie*; Flower stalks: © Adriel Diver

78 Eastern wahoo fruit (top): © Randy Shonkwiler§; Flowers: © Stephen Cresswell

79 Scarlet oak fall foliage (top): © Katja Schulz*; Edwards' hairstreak butterfly: © Dan Hayes

80 Mayapple: © Uli Lorimer

82 Carolina spring beauty (top): © Dan Jaffe Wilder; Flower fly: © Mary Anne Borge; Form: © Uli Lorimer

83 Large-flowered bellwort flower (top): © Dan Jaffe Wilder; Leaves: © Lisa Looke

84 Red baneberry fruit (top): © Lisa Looke; Flowers: © Dan Jaffe Wilder

85 Virginia bluebell flowers (top): © Alan Cressler ; Leaves: © Uli Lorimer

86 Blue lobelia flowers (bottom): © Dan Jaffe Wilder

87 Bumble bee on white snakeroot © Dan Jaffe Wilder; Bog goldenrod © Ed Morris

88 Orange jewelweed flower (top): © Lisa Looke

89 Northern lady fern: © Dan Jaffe Wilder ; Broad beech fern: © Uli Lorimer

90 Sweet azalea flower (top): © Fritz Flohr Reynolds**; Form: © Dan Jaffe Wilder

91 Yellow buckeye flowers (top): by Yann Kemper, Public Domain; Bark: © The Morton Arboretum; Fruit: © biomania (inaturalist.org)

93 Small carpenter bee on New England aster: © Colleen Prieto

95 Buck moth caterpillar: © Steve Krotzer

Index of Native Plant Species